THE SOUTH LANCASHIRE TRAMWAYS COMPANY 1900-1958

By
E.K.Stretch.
Revised and updated by
Ted Gray.

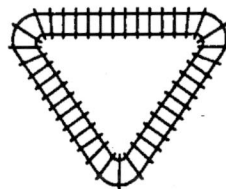

Triangle Publishing

Copyright @ E.K.Stretch c1972
Revised by E.Gray 2006
First Published in 2006 by Triangle Publishing.
British Library Cataloguing in Publication Data.
Stretch/Gray
The South Lancashire Tramways Company Ltd.
ISBN 09550030 24
Printed in England by the Amadeus Press,
Cleckheaton.
Maps by Alan Palmer.
Compiled and edited for publication
by D.J.Sweeney.
Cover design by Scene, Print & Design,
Leigh, Lancs.
Designed and published by
Triangle Publishing,
509, Wigan Road,
Leigh, Lancs. WN7 5HN.
Tel: 01942/677919
www.trianglepublishing.co.uk

Front cover. Car No.69 stands in Market Street, Leigh, ready to work the route to Lowton St. Mary's. In the middle distance is ex-Farnworth bogie-car No.51 on the Bolton service.

Jackson & Son, commercial postcard.

Rear cover. Although 24 top-covered cars had been purchased in 1906 for the additional routes now opened, in its early days the Atherton-Swinton route seems to have been the province of the older open-top trams. Car No.18, destination Swinton, pauses at Mosley Common.

Frontispiece, below. Between 1888 and 1900 the tramway in Farnworth was leased and operated by Edmund Holden, whose horse-drawn vehicles worked from Bolton through Moses Gate and along Manchester Road and Market Street as far as the *Black Horse Hotel*. The three-horse tramcar illustrated is of Eades' Patent Reversible type, as used by the Manchester Carriage and Tramways Company, built at the Company's works at Pendleton. It is seen at Victoria Square in 1897.

CONTENTS

AUTHOR'S NOTE TO THE 1972 EDITION

The interest in tramways and their history has grown up only as tramways themselves have virtually disappeared in this country. In recent years detailed histories of several tramway undertakings have appeared, but these have dealt almost solely with municipal tramways. The company undertakings have been sadly neglected. This is possibly because their history tends tobe more involved, but principally because sources of information are not so easy to find. The Minutes of Corporation committees are available for all to consult; the discussions at Council meetings are reported in considerable detail in the local Press. The deliberations of Boards of Directors are carried out behind closed doors; the annual reports to shareholders are concerned with financial results rather than details of operation; the local Press is a less fruitful source of information because it has no long committee discussions to report and because Company undertakings covered, in general, a more extensive area so that several different newspapers need to be consulted to unearth details of happenings on different parts of the system. The S.L.T., unlike some tramway companies, continued to exist after the tramways had been abandoned, and there was a continuity of existence with the former Lancashire United Transport. Nevertheless, official records of the tramway period have for the most part been destroyed long since, and the principal sources of information for accurate details in this history have had to be the local newspaper files.

In one or two cases, dates given in this book differ from those published elsewhere; all dates given, however, have been carefully checked with contemporary sources, and can confidently be stated to be accurate; where there is any doubt, this has been stated.

The electric tramway was the first successful form of cheap door-to-door transport; the S.L.T. may not have made much money for its shareholders in the first twenty years, but it played a vital part in the development of the district it served. I hope that this account will be read not only by transport enthusiasts but also by local people interested in the past development of their home district, and I would beg the indulgence of the former for occasionally explaining terms well understood by them but little known to persons not interested in transport.

This account could not have been written without the assistance of many people over the years, and to single out a few by name in no way means that I am ungrateful to the rest. I would like particularly to thank Mr. J. C. Gillham of London for considerable help in the early stages of the research; the late Mr. Walter Gratwicke of London for information on rolling stock, and Mr. W. H. Bett of Birmingham for most of the information on tickets. For help with specific points I would like to thank Mr. J. H. Price, Mr. N. N. Forbes, Mr. A. Ralphs, Mr. E. R.Pollard, Mr. E. Gray and Mr. A. Winstan Bond, as well as several officers of Lancashire United Transport, particularly Mr. Lloyd, former Traffic Manager, and Mr. T. B. Boothroyd, former Chief Inspector. The account could never have been compiled at all without the files of local newspapers and similar documents in the public libraries of Leigh, Bolton, Wigan, and St.Helens, and the story of the Farnworth Council Tramways would have been much less complete if the Town Clerk's Department of Farnworth Corporation had not unearthed for me some years ago a long-lost book of Press Cuttings. Deposited Plans and Acts of Parliament were consulted in the County Records Office at Preston: Ordnance Survey 25-inch plans were studied in Cambridge University Library, and of course provided much useful information about track layout. Last but not least, the Manchester Transport Museum Society, through its Curator, Mr. C. Taylor, made available numerous volumes of *Tramway & Railway World.*

Thanks are also due to the various photographers who have allowed use of their photographs: it has not always been possible to trace the origin of photos, and apologies are tendered to any photographer whose pictures have inadvertently been used without permission or credited mistakenly to someone else.

E.K.Stretch

PREFACE TO THE 2006 EDITION

Keith Stretch grew up in the South Lancashire Tramways operating area, and was passionately interested in tramways and trolleybuses. He published his history of the South Lancashire system in 1972 and also completed a similar work on the tramways of St. Helens and Wigan. A schoolmaster by profession, he taught in Newcastle-under-Lyme. On his untimely death, he bequeathed his rights to his published work to the Manchester Transport Museum Society, the voluntary organization of transport enthusiasts, which had been responsible for the production of the South Lancashire and Wigan volumes. The South Lancashire Tramways history has long been out of print, and this new edition has been kindly facilitated by Dennis Sweeney of Triangle Publishing in order to form a companion volume to *A Trolleybus to the Punch Bowl* by Phillip Taylor. For the purposes of this revised work, Keith Stretch's original text of the tramway chapters has been left largely unaltered, although the opportunity has been taken to incorporate some new material and to make some corrections which had been identified by Keith himself. The trolleybus section of the original work has been omitted, as this is fully covered in other publications.

The number of illustrations has been greatly increased, since many more have come to light since the original printing in 1972, and new captions have been written. All the illustrations come from the collections of Arthur Kirby and Edward Gray, and the original photographer or source is credited where known. Apologies are offered for any inadvert omissions.

The story of the South Lancashire Tramway Company's involvement in trolleybus and (as Lancashire United Transport) motor bus operation has been touched on only briefly in this volume, as full details may be found in the following publications:-

Lancashire United by Eric Ogden.
    (Transport Publishing Company 1974)
British Bus & Trolleybus Systems No.7:
Lancashire United by Eric Ogden.
    (Transport Publishing Company 1985)
Looking Back at Lancashire United by Phillip Higgs.
    (Lancastrian Transport Publications 1996)
A Trolleybus to the Punch Bowl by Phillip Taylor.
    (Triangle Publishing 2002)

Although the South Lancashire Tramways Company had abandoned its tramways and converted to trolleybus and motor bus operation by the end of 1933, for the sake of completion, brief details of the subsequent history of the tramcars which survived to pass into Bolton ownership have been included, together with reference to the final years of trolleybus operation. This edition has been prepared with new illustrations and captions by Edward Gray. Acknowledgement is made to Roy Brook for his advice and expertise in the matter of tramcar manufacturers. Alan Palmer has re-drawn the original maps and track plans to his usual high standard.

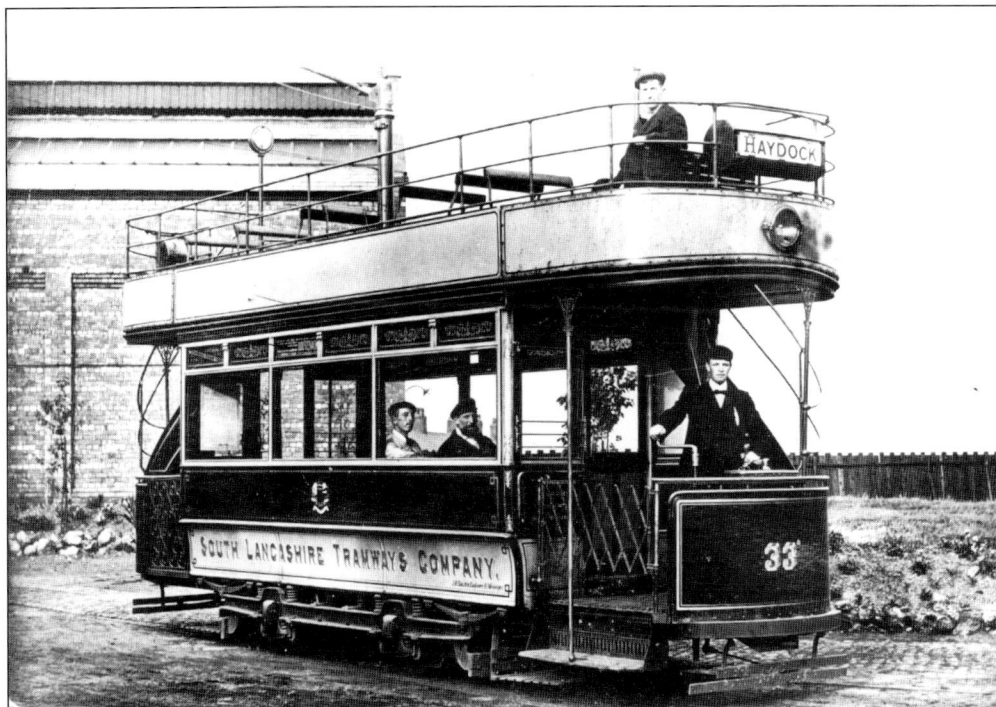

Plate 1. The first 45 tramcars ordered by the new company were supplied by G.F.Milnes. They were single-truck open-top vehicles seating 22 on longitudinal benches on the lower deck (11 each side) and 33 on reversible garden seats on top, total 55. The Company's literature announced with pride that car No.45 had upholstered seats in the lower saloon. Car No.33 is seen at Atherton Depot yard in original condition, with fully lined-out livery and the full company title on the rocker panel. The rotating indicator boards were later replaced by roller blind destination screens. The platform gates fell into disuse, and were eventually removed.

S.L.T. –
TRAMWAYS AUTHORISED
AND CONNECTIONS?

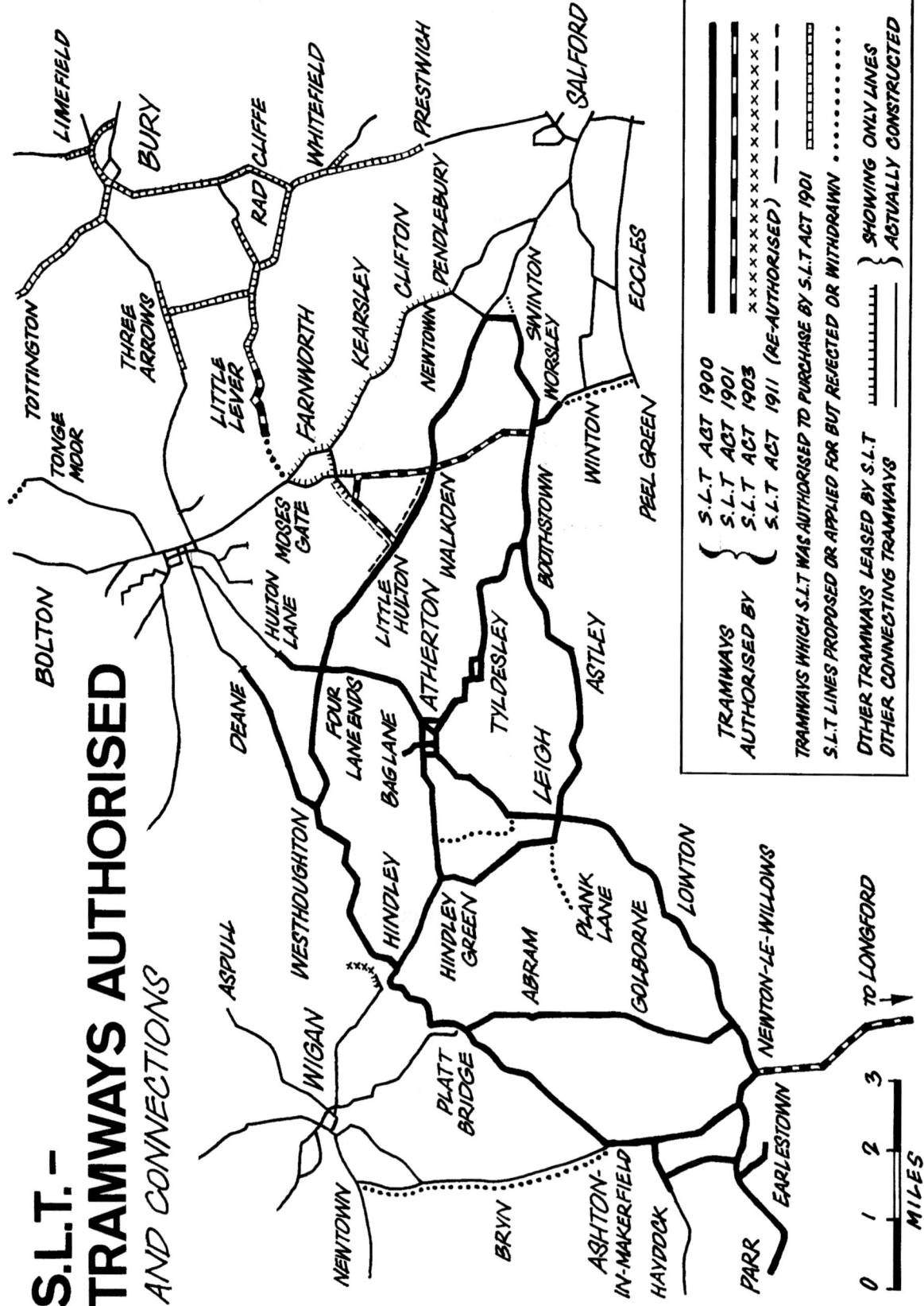

Map legend:

Tramways Authorised by	{ S.L.T ACT 1900, S.L.T ACT 1901, S.L.T ACT 1903, S.L.T ACT 1911 (RE-AUTHORISED)

TRAMWAYS WHICH S.L.T WAS AUTHORISED TO PURCHASE BY S.L.T ACT 1901

S.L.T LINES PROPOSED OR APPLIED FOR BUT REJECTED OR WITHDRAWN ·····

OTHER TRAMWAYS LEASED BY S.L.T } SHOWING ONLY LINES
OTHER CONNECTING TRAMWAYS } ACTUALLY CONSTRUCTED

Locations shown: LIMEFIELD, BURY, RADCLIFFE, WHITEFIELD, PRESTWICH, SALFORD, TOTTINGTON, THREE ARROWS, LITTLE LEVER, FARNWORTH, KEARSLEY, CLIFTON, NEWTOWN, PENDLEBURY, SWINTON, WORSLEY, ECCLES, TONGE MOOR, MOSES GATE, HULTON LANE, LITTLE HULTON, WALKDEN, WINTON, PEEL GREEN, BOLTON, DEANE, FOUR LANE ENDS, BAG LANE, ATHERTON, BOOTHSTOWN, ASTLEY, TYLDESLEY, LEIGH, ASPULL, WESTHOUGHTON, HINDLEY, PLANK LANE, LOWTON, WIGAN, PLATT BRIDGE, HINDLEY GREEN, ABRAM, GOLBORNE, NEWTON-LE-WILLOWS?, NEWTOWN, BRYN, ASHTON-IN-MAKERFIELD, EARLESTOWN, HAYDOCK, PARR, TO LONGFORD

0 1 2 3 MILES

6

CHAPTER 1. EARLY PLANS

The background

The standard-gauge electric tramways of South Lancashire formed the largest connected network in Great Britain. Totalling about 500 route miles, they reached from Liverpool in the west to beyond Manchester in the east, crossing the Cheshire border to Stalybridge and Stockport, and extending northwards to Bolton, Bury, Rochdale, and Bacup, at which latter town connection was made with the four-foot gauge tramways running north-westwards to Accrington and Blackburn, totalling a futher 34 miles.

Of this vast network, the South Lancashire Tramways Company's system, totalling $39\frac{1}{2}$ route miles (of which nearly 9 miles were leased from local authorities) formed only a small part, though it was a vital link without which the network would have remained in several detached portions. Nevertheless, the Company's system was the largest company-owned electric tramway system outside London. Many others carried heavier traffic and owned more tramcars, but none operated so great a route mileage. The extensive 3ft 6in gauge network of the Birmingham and Midland Tramways Joint Committee was much larger, but was made of the undertakings of several associated companies, each of which retained its legal independence, and none of which was as large as the S.L.T. in terms of route mileage. The S.L.T. itself, of course, was part of a smaller, similar group, controlled at first by the South Lancashire Electric Traction and Power Company Ltd., and later by Lancashire United Tramways Ltd. At its maximum, from 1913 to 1919, this group was responsible for the operation of $61\frac{1}{4}$ miles of tramways. If all the lines authorised had been built, however, the S.L.T. alone would have owned nearly 76 miles, while the grand total authorised to all the undertakings which were eventually owned or operated by the group was $114\frac{1}{2}$ miles.

As one of the most densely populated and industrialised areas of the country, it is natural that interurban tramways in South Lancashire were proposed at an early date, as soon as mechanical traction had begun to succeed the horse. At a superficial glance, the whole area appears to be well provided with railways, but in fact many of the smaller towns were poorly served, for their stations were often inconveniently situated, and while it is true that some of the principal lines were built very early, railway construction in the area continued into the twentieth century, and as late as the 1870s there were considerable gaps.

Horse tramways made their appearance in Liverpool in 1869, and Manchester and Salford in 1877; in Bolton and Wigan in 1880, and St. Helens in 1881. Northwards from Manchester a considerable mileage of steam tramways, operated by the Manchester Bury Rochdale and Oldham company was developed from 1883 onwards, and steam replaced horses in Wigan in 1883 and in St. Helens in 1890. While most of the tramways in South Lancashire were of standard (4ft 8$\frac{1}{2}$in) gauge, the 3ft 6in gauge had been adopted in Wigan and for some of the routes of the M.B.R. & 0 system. The first electric tram services in the area began in Liverpool at the end of 1898; electric trams began to operate in St. Helens in July 1899, and in Bolton in December 1899. Other undertakings quickly followed suit.

In some cases, electric tramways were firmly proposed two years or more before they actually came into operation, for obtaining the necessary powers, as well as the actual work of electrification, was quite a lengthy process. The first electric tram actually to run in South Lancashire would seem to have been a small single-deck car, drawing its power from a conduit placed beneath the running rails, and not from an overhead wire, which was demonstrated to the Press on a short length of track in the Prescot works of the British Insulated Wire Company on 9th March 1897.

In the towns of Leigh and Atherton, which were later to become the centre of the South Lancashire Tramways Company's network, there were proposals in 1896 for a "Leigh and Atherton District Tramways Company" to construct 3ft 6in gauge electric tramways from Lowton St. Mary's station to Atherton Central station, via Leigh and Atherton, together with branches from Leigh to Plank Lane and from Leigh along Chapel Street to the corner of Green Lane, Bedford. This scheme was dropped after a dispute with Leigh Urban District Council over the posting of various notices without the consent of the Council, although general agreement had been reached on most matters. This was the second scheme for the area to come to nothing, for in 1882 Mr. A. Speight of St. Helens, who had been the contractor responsible for the construction of the first horse tram routes in St. Helens, had proposed horse tramways for Leigh and Atherton. However, it was not long before the two towns were involved in yet another scheme.

With the growth of tramways in South Lancashire and the first vague proposals for electrification, a number of businessmen had become interested in the possibilities for interurban tramways, not only for passenger traffic, but for freight traffic, and the Liverpool Chamber of Trade encouraged the preparation of various schemes to connect the Liverpool docks directly with most of the principal cotton spinning towns of South-east Lancashire. Among the schemes proposed was one by a Mr. John T. Wood

Plate 2. A well-loaded car No.27 makes a trial trip through Leigh before the commencement of services in 1902 and is seen at the 'Turnpike,' the junction of Railway Road, King Street, Market Street and Bradshawgate. The top deck appears full to capacity, and both staircase and platform offer vantage points for others. The motorman does not wear a uniform and is likely to be a Company official.

The picture makes an interesting comparison with the scene at this location today. The building with the domed roof and flagpole atop is still extant today as Barclay's Bank. The Town Hall building, constructed in 1905, which included the complete frontage of shops and upper accommodation, replaced the the buildings on the right hand side, as viewed, of Market Street. The site on the corner of Market Street and Railway Road, where the property with a lower roof level stands, is now occupied by National Westminster Bank.

Plate 3. The first route opened for service was the section from Four Lane Ends to Lowton, ready by 20th October 1902. Car No.17, bound for Lowton, pauses for the photographer at Pennington in late 1902. A poster in the end window advertises a 'Grand Charity Football' match between a South Lancashire Tramways team and opponents from Westleigh. In the centre window a second poster advises passengers that 'THIS CAR STOPS AT OHMY'S CIRCUS.' *T.Boothroyd.*

which proposed electric tramways (or possibly steam on certain sections) linking Liverpool with St. Helens and thence to Leigh, Atherton, Farnworth, Whitefield and Oldham.

Lancashire Light Railways Company formed

Something similar to Mr. Wood's proposals first achieved more definite shape with the formation of the St. Helens, Leigh & Bolton Light Railways Syndicate, which was quickly transformed into the Lancashire Light Railways Company Limited, registered on 21st April 1898, with a capital of £50,000 and offices at 12 St. John's Lane, Liverpool. The promoters of this company were the brothers Jacob Atherton, of Gateacre, and James Basnett Atherton, of Manhattan House, Rainhill. Both were said to have considerable experience of tramway operation and construction in England and abroad, but in fact their experience must have been principally with horse tramways. Jacob, the younger brother, born in 1852, was chairman of the South-Eastern Metropolitan Tramways Company (a small horse tramway system in the Lewisham area). James was managing director of the British Insulated Wire Co., Ltd., of Prescot, a company formed by the brothers on their return from the U.S.A. in 1890, and already mentioned in connection with the experimental conduit car demonstrated in 1897. At the end of 1897, both brothers had obtained financial control of the St.Helens & District Tramways Co., Ltd., which operated (but no longer owned) the steam tramways based on St. Helens. The Secretary of the L.L.R. was Mr. G. Saies, who was also Secretary of the St.Helens & District, and of several Australian electricity companies*, and later of the Llanelly & District Traction Company: the Atherton brothers were directors of most of these companies.

The Lancashire Light Railways Company proposed to build two separate electric tramways. They were to be of standard gauge, and it was proposed to carry goods traffic between 11.00 p.m. and 5.00 a.m., when passenger cars would not be running. Though the lines were to be built under the Light Railways Acts to gain certain legal advantages, principally concerned with liability to local rates and with the alignment of tracks, they would in fact be ordinary street tramways.

It is interesting to note that one of the Atherton brothers' companies was the Electric Supply Company of Victoria Ltd., which acquired in 1899 and 1902 respectively the tramway systems of Bendigo and Ballarat, electrified in 1903 and 1905, these two systems continued to operate until 1972 and 1971 respectively, under the control of the Victorian State Electricity Commission since 1931. Although regular public services in Ballarat and Bendigo ceased in the early 1970s, a section of each system is still operated as a tourist attraction.

The Liverpool and Prescot Light Railway, 3 miles 9 chains in length, was to link the authorised Liverpool Corporation tram terminus on the then city boundary at Knotty Ash with the proposed St. Helens tram terminus at Brook Bridge, Prescot (this extension from the centre of Prescot was authorised by the St. Helens Corporation Act of 12th August 1898). A Light Railway Order for the Liverpool and Prescot was obtained in May 1898, and confirmed by the Board of Trade on 10th March 1899. However, the line was not constructed until 1902, and was then worked as part of the St. Helens Tramways. It is described in Appendix II.

The St. Helens, Leigh and Bolton Light Railways were to consist of a line running from the proposed St. Helens terminus at the *Horse Shoe Hotel*, Parr (authorised August 1898) via Newton-le-Willows, Lowton St. Mary's, Leigh, and Atherton, to the intended Bolton Corporation tram terminus at Middle Hulton (Hulton Lane). A further connection with the St.Helens tramways would be by a line from Newton via Ashton Road to Haydock (*Ram's Head*), and there were also to be branches from Atherton to Hindley, and from Atherton through Tyldesley to the Tyldesley/Worsley boundary at Stirrup Bridge, Boothstown. The plans for these lines, totalling 23 miles 75 chains, were deposited on 30th November 1898. Agreement was reached with most of the local authorities concerned, subject to the reconstruction of certain sections of road and the provision of street lighting by the company, but the scheme was suddenly withdrawn in September 1899: in view of the Company's relatively small capital for such a length of line, one may well wonder whether the scheme was really intended seriously.

It had not been entirely unopposed, for a public meeting at Newton had indignantly protested that the tramways would spoil 'the prettiest village in England'(!) On the whole, however, the abandonment of the scheme was a considerable disappointment to most of the towns and villages concerned, who had welcomed the plan as "likely to break the railway monopoly".

A link between the two separate parts of the proposed undertaking was of course provided by the St. Helens tramways, electrification of which had been decided upon in October 1897. These had been owned by the Corporation since 1st April 1897, and the Atherton brothers and their associates planned successfully to retain control of the operation of those tramways and their projected extensions by forming a new company - the New St. Helens & District Tramways Company Ltd., registered 4th November 1898 -to provide and operate electric cars. No difficulty was anticipated, therefore, in operating through St. Helens, but in fact, as will be seen later, the Corporation did not welcome the prospect of through traffic, particularly through freight traffic.

The South Lancashire Tramways Act 1900

The disappointment caused by the abandonment of the St. Helens, Leigh and Bolton scheme proved only temporary, for at the end of 1899 the same promoters, together with one William Marriner Brigg, revived the scheme with several additions. This time they promoted a private Bill, to which the Royal Assent was eventually given on 6th August 1900 (63&64 Vict., cap-ccxliii) This Act incorporated the South Lancashire Tramways Company, with an authorised capital of £1,100,000 in £10 shares, and to borrow a further £366,000. The Company was authorised to construct 62 miles 52.33 chains of standard gauge electric tramway, of which 21 miles 72.77 chains were to be double track, and 40 miles 59.96 chains single track. So involved were the various incidental works such as street widenings, and the various agreements with local authorities, that the Act fills over 150 pages. The tramways were listed in 44 lengths numbered from 1 to 28, and were claimed to be the largest mileage ever authorised by a single Act. They comprised the following routes:

(i) From a junction with the St. Helens tramways at Haydock (*Ram's Head*) via Ashton-in-Makerfield, Platt Bridge, Hindley, Atherton, Tyldesley, Boothstown, and Worsley, to Swinton Market Place, with a short branch along Partington Lane to Swinton Church: total 18½ miles. (Tramways Nos. 12,13,15,16,17, 3,6,7,8,9,10 and 22).

(ii) From a junction with the above line near the *Plough Inn,* Hindley, to Swinton Church, via Westhoughton, Chequerbent, Hulton Lane Ends, Little Hulton, and Walkden:1½ miles. (Tramways Nos. 19 and 21).

(iii) From the St. Helens boundary near Parr (to which a St. Helens extension from the *Horse Shoe* was authorised the same day), passing near Earlestown and then through Newton-le-Willows, Lowton St. Mary's, Leigh, Atherton, and Hulton Lane Ends to a junction with the authorised Bolton Corporation line at the south end of Hulton Lane: 14 miles. This was the same as the 'main line' of the abandoned St. Helens, Leigh, and Bolton scheme. (Tramways Nos. 1, 2, 4, and 5).

(iv) A connecting line along Vista Road, between (i) near *Ram's Head* and (iii) near Earlestown: 1m 9ch. (Tramway No. 23).

(v) A short branch to Earlestown railway station: 50ch. (Tramway No. 24).

(vi) From Old Boston corner, between Haydock and Ashton on line (i), to Newton on line (iii) via Lodge Lane and Ashton Road: 1¼ miles. (Tramway No. 25).

(vii) From Lowton L. & N.W.R. station, on line (iii) to Platt Bridge on line (i) via Golborne and Abram: 4½ miles. (Tramway No. 26).

(viii) From Hindley Green, between Hindley and Atherton, via Tamar to Leigh, and then via Astley to Boothstown: 7¾ miles. (Tramways Nos. 27 and 28).

(ix) From Westhoughton to a junction with the Bolton Corporation line near the north end of Hulton Lane, Deane: 2¼ miles (Tramway No. 20).

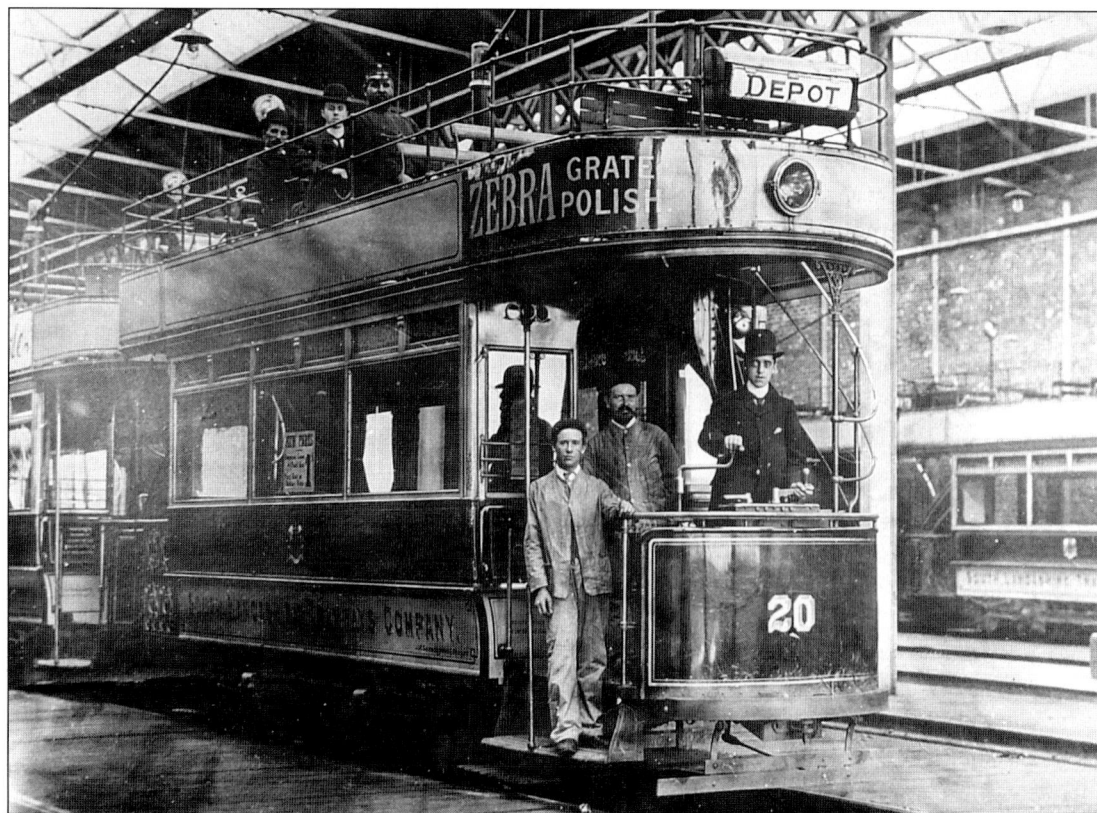

Plate 4. Members of the shed staff pose for the photographer on car No.20 in Atherton Depot about 1902. The depot was built to house 50 tramcars. *G.Murcott.*

(x) From the centre of Atherton to Bag Lane station: 46 chains (Tramways 18 and 18b).

(xi) From line (i) at Worsley Court House to a junction with the authorised Eccles tramway on the Worsley/Eccles boundary at Winton: 55 chains. (Tramway No. 11).

The other tramways in the Act, numbered with suffix letters, (for example 8a, 8b, 8c) were connecting curves and junction lines between the tramways mentioned above.

Although many people imagine South Lancashire to be one huge built-up area, and a 1901 prospectus claims "along most of the authorised route there is an almost continuous line of houses" this was by no means true at the time, and though one must admit that industry and housing were rarely completely out of sight, there was still a considerable amount of open country between the towns which it was planned to serve. Some ribbon development followed the tramways, but even thirty years later some sections were still rural - principally between Haydock and Ashton, Boothstown and Worsley, Atherton and Hulton Lane Ends, and Swinton and Walkden. On some of the planned lines which in the end were never built, even this ribbon development did not take place. However, since 1950 there has been considerable housing development in the area, principally at Hindley, at Little Hulton and Walkden, and north of Tyldesley and Atherton, while many long-familiar views have been altered by motorway construction and by reconstruction in town centres, but only now can the claim in the prospectus be said even to approach the truth.

The 1900 Act was not obtained without lengthy negotiations with local authorities and other bodies, and the opposition had been overcome only by considerable concessions. The Company was forced to agree to provide free electric street lighting over the whole of its routes, and to carry out various extensive road and bridge works and improvements - no less than 61 such works are listed in the Act. In some cases these involved the demolition and rebuilding of property, for instance a public house in Tyldesley, and a public hall, "Church House" in Atherton. All roads along which the trams ran were to be widened to 27 feet, including pavements, though in fact this was not carried out everywhere. Considerable consternation was caused amongst local authorities in July when all the road improvement clauses were struck out during the Committee stage of the Bill. They were restored after the local authorities had protested that the whole scheme was thus rendered "of no value", a comment which shows that they were more concerned to have road improvements carried out at someone else's expense than about the benefits which improved transport would bring.

Local authorities were to be allowed the free use of the tracks at night for the carriage of house refuse, road materials, etc., by horse traction. In fact, none of the authorities ever used these powers.

Leigh Corporation* was one of the most vehement opponents of the Bill, but eventually agreed to the Company's proposals on condition that if the Corporation should ever operate tramways itself, it should have free running powers over the S.L.T. lines within the borough. Further, the Corporation insisted that in return for agreeing to the construction of the through St. Helens - Leigh - Bolton line, the other lines in Leigh, namely to Boothstown via Astley and to Hindley Green via Tamar, should not be constructed within the borough without specific written consent from the Corporation. The Company was not to oppose the Corporation's seeking powers for the same lines. However, as the Company's power station and depot were to be built on a piece of land adjoining Pilling Street, off Twist Lane on the Hindley Green line, the Corporation's consent was not required to the construction of this line as far as the Depot, provided that passengers were not carried on it.

Worsley Urban District Council, which administered both Worsley and Walkden and had its offices and Town Hall at Walkden, had originally in January 1900, welcomed the S.L.T. plans subject to various minor conditions, but later opposed them on the ground that the tramways would not be for the benefit of the district but were being constructed for long-distance through traffic, and there were even public protest meetings against the Company's 'monopolising our tramways'. However, agreement was finally reached, and one cannot help feeling that a good deal of the opposition was a bluff to wring further concessions out of the Company. The Company agreed, amongst other things, to grant running

*Leigh had become a Borough in October 1899. As an administrative unit it had existed only since 1875, when the Local Board Districts of Pennington, Bedford, and Westleigh were amalgamated to form Leigh Local Board District, which became an Urban District in 1894.

Plate 5. Car No.35 working the Lowton service, has just passed beneath the LNWR line at Howe Bridge Station, between Atherton and Leigh.

Formation of the S.L.E.T & P. Co., Ltd.

Although the Act had been passed, there was difficulty in raising the capital, and no construction work began. On 29th November 1900 another company was registered, the South Lancashire Electric Traction and Power Company Ltd., with a capital of £850,000 in £1.00 shares, of which £600,000 were 6% preference shares. The new company acquired the whole of the shares of the Lancashire Light Railways and South Lancashire Tramways companies, as well as those of a third company, South Lancashire Electric Supply Co., Ltd., which had been registered on 29th June 1900. The offices of the new company, like its existing three subsidiaries, were at 12 St. John's Lane, Liverpool, (transferred early in 1904 to 9 North John St), and the two Atherton brothers were directors. The other directors were the Hon. Arthur Stanley, the Hon. Stanley, and Messrs. Joseph Beecham and E.K.Muspratt. Sir J.A.Willox was chairman: he was already chairman of the New St. Helens & District Tramways Company. The Hon. Arthur Stanley succeeded him as chairman of the S.L.E.T. & P.Co., in 1902.

By counting twice the sections authorised as double track, the new company's prospectus made the S.L.T.s authorised system seem distinctly larger than it was in fact. The new company proposed to extend and co-ordinate more closely the activities of its subsidiaries, and it was intended that this acquisition by a single owning company would ensure that such co-operation would remain permanent. It was proposed to seek powers for a further 23 miles 60 chains of tramway.

Of this total, 9 miles 26 chains would be known as the Bolton, Turton, and Darwen Light Railways, and would be the property of Lancashire Light Railways. Completely isolated from the rest of the S.L.T; and Lancashire Light Railways, the Bolton, Turton and Darwen lines would link the Bolton Corporation tramways at Dunscar and Tonge Moor with the 4ft gauge Darwen CorporationTramways at Darwen Cemetery, and there would be a short branch to Bromley Cross Station and a longer one from Egerton to a point near Belmont. Although plans were deposited on 30th November 1900, it is not surprising that this wildly optimistic scheme was soon dropped, for the sparse population and the steep gradients were hardly suitable for economic tramway operation. A more detailed description appears in Appendix III.

Plate 8. Car No.38, en-route for Atherton, negotiates Elliott Street, Tyldesley. On single track sections with side-mounted bracket arms supporting the overhead wire, the off-set trolley-pole sometimes had a considerable sideways reach to make contact with the power supply.

Barrett & Co.

14

The remaining 14½ miles proposed were S.L.T. property. Two lines were proposed within the borough of Leigh: one of these, about three-quarters of a mile long, would begin at the "Sportsman Inn", at the corner of Twist Lane and Wigan Road on the authorised Hindley Green line, and extend along Firs Lane and Plank Lane as far as Plank Lane Colliery. This line had been surveyed in October 1900, and at the same time the Company tried to obtain from Leigh Corporation the permission required under the 1900 Act to construct the Astley and Hindley Green lines. In September, the Corporation had appointed a Committee to investigate the possibilities of the Corporation constructing and working its own tramways, or constructing its own tramways and leasing them to the Company, or allowing the Company to construct and work the tramways. As a result, the Corporation refused to grant permission for the time being. The Company then added another line to its proposals. This was about 1¼ miles long, and would run along Kirkhall Lane and Westleigh Lane to a junction with the Atherton-Hindley line at Dangerous Corner. The Company tried to dissuade the Corporation from building tramways and suggested the appointment of a joint committee to administer the Plank Lane, Hindley Green, Dangerous Corner and Astley lines. The Company would operate these lines, but the accounts would be kept separate. When the Corporation requested "more definite proposals", the Company offered 15% of the net receipts to the Corporation, increasing to 20% after five years. The Corporation would have the right to purchase after 14 years. However, the Corporation finally decided that these terms were not satisfactory, and resolved definitely to refuse permission for construction of the Hindley Green and Astley lines. Annoyed at this, the Company wrote to the Corporation on 8th March 1901, stating that if the Corporation would not agree to the construction of these lines, the Company "might feel compelled to consider building its generating station outside the borough."

South Lancashire Tramways Act 1901

The two additional Leigh lines, to Plank Lane and Dangerous Corner, had to be withdrawn from the S.L.T. Bill at the request of Leigh Corporation. As passed on 17th August 1901 (1 Edw. VII,cap. cclvii.) the Act authorised 12 miles 40 chains of tramway, of which 7 miles 63 chains were to be single track, 4 miles 23 chains double, and 34 chains tramroad. This comprised the following lines (the numbering given here is as used in the Act)

(1)   From a junction with the Liverpool and Prescot Light Railways at Huyton Lane, to a junction with the Liverpool Corporation Tramways at Broad Green, via Huyton Lane, Archway Road, Roby Road, and Broad Green Road. (3 miles 27 chains, of which 10 chains on private right of way).

(2)   From Newton-le-Willows through Winwick to a junction with the authorised Warrington Corporation Tramways at the Warrington boundary, Longford. (3 miles 45 chains).

(3)   Along the direct road (Walkden Road and Memorial Road) from Worsley Church to Walkden Memorial, and onwards along Bolton Road and Worsley Road to a junction with Farnworth Council Tramways (under construction) on the Farnworth boundary at Brookhouse. (2 miles 56 chains)

(4)   From a junction with the authorised Hindley-Westhoughton-Swinton line at Little Hulton, along Cleggs Lane to the authorised Farnworth tramways on the boundary at Buckley Lane End (64 chains).

(5)   A tramroad, 34 chains long, joining Buckley Lane End and Brookhouse without entering Farnworth.

(6)   Through Little Lever from the Farnworth boundary at Farnworth Bridge to the Radcliffe boundary at Stopes, thus linking the intended Farnworth U.D.C. and Radcliffe U.D.C.tramways. (1 mile 54 chains).

Tramway No. 1 would be isolated from the rest of the S.L.T. by several miles, though connected with the Lancashire Light Railways. Like most of the tramways in this Act, it was never built, though the line built by Liverpool Corporation in 1914 from Broad Green to Bowring Park followed much the same course as the western part of this tramway. Tramway No. 6 was also isolated from the rest of the S.L.T. The company was required to build a road along the course of Tramway No, 5. Lines Nos. 3 and 6 were often referred to as the "Bury-Eccles" tramway, a misleading and somewhat "imperialist" title. Both lines had been introduced as a result of an agreement with Worsley U.D.C. in 1900: the 1900 Act had included a clause that powers for these lines should be sought in the next parliamentary session. Originally the Little Lever line was intended to extend to Prestwich, but in the interval between the 1900 and 1901 Acts, Whitefield and Radcliffe Urban District Councils had successfully applied for powers for the sections between Stopes and Prestwich.

The 1901 Act also authorised the Company to enter into agreements concerning running powers with Liverpool Corporation and Warrington Corporation. Farnworth Council was granted running powers from Buckley Lane End to Little Hulton, Little Hulton to Walkden, and Walkden to Brookhouse, in return for which the S.L.T. was granted running powers over all the Farnworth tramways.

The S.L.T. was empowered to arrange running powers over, or to purchase, or to lease, the Radcliffe U.D.C. tramways, and the Whitefield U.D.C. tramways (authorised 1900), and the tramways authorised by the Bury and District Tramways Order 1881. The Company was also authorised to construct any unconstructed lines authorised by the Whitefield and Radcliffe Tramway Orders. If the Company merely obtained running powers in Radcliffe and Whitefield, and did not purchase or lease these systems, then Radcliffe U.D.C. was to have running powers in Little Lever, and also over those lines of Farnworth U.D.C. and Whitefield U.D.C. for which the Company possessed running powers. The lines authorised by the Bury and District Tramways Order of 1881 totalled 8 miles 72.45 chains, forming part of the extensive steam-operated system of the Bury, Rochdale, and Oldham Tramways Company. 5 miles 66.65 chains, from BroughtonToll on the main Manchester and Bury Road, via Prestwich, Whitefield, and Blackford Bridge to Bury Market Place, were standard-gauge; the remainder, consisting of the lines from Bury toTottington and from Bury along Walmersley Road to Hamilton Street, Limefield, and also the first half mile of the line from Bury to Heywood and Rochdale, were 3ft 6in gauge. The Whitefield U.D.C. Tramways Order authorised the electrification of that part of the Broughton to Bury line situated in Whitefield, together with one or two additional branches, while the Radcliffe U.D.C. Tramways Order authorised 8 miles 18 chains of line, from Stopes through Radcliffe and along New Road to the Whitefield boundary (connecting with a new branch authorised by the Whitefield Order), and along Cross Lane and Dumers Lane to the Bury boundary; from Radcliffe to the Bolton and Bury Road at Three Arrows, and along the Bolton and Bury Road for the $1\frac{1}{2}$ miles that it lay in the Radcliffe U.D. area. As the S.L.T. line from Farnworth through Little Lever to Stopes was never built, none of the Company's powers in this area were ever exercised. The Radcliffe tramways came to be worked by Bury, while the electrification of the former steam tramways, and widening to standard-gauge where necessary, was carried out by the local authorites in their own districts, though only Bury Corporation became a tramway operator; the Whitefield U.D.C. and Prestwich U.D.C. lines were leased to Salford, apart from a very short length in Whitefield leased to Radcliffe.

Finally, the 1901 Act authorised the S.L.T. to raise a further £200,000 capital (£150,000 in shares, and £50,000 by loans).

Plate 9. The proposed route from Atherton to Swinton had been completed as far as Tyldesley by October 1902, but it was to be another two-and-a-half years before the eastward extension through Mosley Common to the Tyldesley-Worsley boundary at Stirrup Bridge, Boothstown, was ready. This section opened to traffic on the 20th April 1905. Car No.39 stands at the temporary Boothstown terminus, its trolley turned ready for the return to Atherton. In the road beyond, track to Worsley and Swinton is under construction, though another 18 months would pass before the route was extended.

Plate 10. The photographer has now done an about-turn and captures Car No.30. The car has made use of the crossover and is ready to return to Atherton. The inevitable crowd of onlookers has gathered to watch the proceedings. In the background is the curved gradient of Coupe Brow, scene of a near-disaster in September 1905, when a descending car approaching the terminus overshot the end of the track.

GENERATING STATION & TRAM SHEDS, LEIGH.

Plate 11. The Company chose to build its central depot and power station at Howe Bridge, about half way on Leigh Road (B5215) between Atherton and Leigh. The administrative offices which formed the frontage were added later. The photograph was taken from the south side of Leigh Road, on land subsequently occupied by an extensive motor bus garage. The whole site has since been cleared and housing built.

17

Lancashire United Tramways Ltd.

The new company, Lancashire United Tramways Ltd., was registered on 29th December 1905. This company had the same registered office as the old (9 North John St., Liverpool) and the Hon. Arthur Stanley was Chairman of both. Three other directors - Edwin Adam, Joseph Beecham, and Robert Walton - were on the boards of both companies, but at this point the Atherton brothers disappear from the scene. Jacob died in Torquay in December 1921 having survived his elder brother by some years.

By a contract signed on 2nd January 1906, the undertaking of the S.L.E.T. & P. Co., Ltd. including the shares of the S.L.T. and L.L.R. companies, and also the inactive South Lancashire Electric Supply Co., Ltd., was sold to the new L.U.T. The L.U.T. company's authorised capital was £200,000 in Ordinary Shares, and £700,000 in various kinds of debenture; £822,708 was actually issued. A good deal of this was intended to finance the construction of some of the authorised lines which it was felt would provide much-needed connections with other tramway undertakings. It was not, however, intended to construct all the authorised tramways, although the S.L.T. had obtained a fourth Act on 4th August 1905 (5 Edw. VII, cap. cxlviii) which authorised another one-year extension of time for construction of tramways and purchase of lands. This Act also authorised the abandonment of all unconstructed tramways in the borough of Leigh, and the unconstructed line in Hindley from the *Plough Inn* to Castle Hill Road (replaced by the line authorised in the 1903 Act). It was proposed to absorb the Lancashire Light Railways undertaking into the S.L.T., but this proposal was withdrawn owing to the opposition of St. Helens Corporation.

Up to this time, capital expenditure on the S.L.T. system had amounted to £508,104, including £151,903 on permanent way, £62,036 on electrical equipment, £28,122 on rolling-stock, and £102,873 on street works. The high expenditure on street works will be particularly noted. The comparatively low expenditure on electrical equipment, of course, is accounted for by the power station being the property of the owning company instead of the S.L.T. itself.

Plate 21. The driver of car No.6 on Leigh Road, Worsley, wears a non-standard cap, and the inspector standing in the roadway looks suitably serious and dignified for the photographer. In the background is the bridge linking Worsley Old and New Halls.

Commercial postcard.

CHAPTER 3. THE FARNWORTH COUNCIL TRAMWAYS

The first extension under the new regime took place on Sunday, 1st April 1906, when the S.L.T. took over the Farnworth Urban District Council Tramways, and also the tramway owned by Kearsley Urban District Council and operated by Farnworth. The combined undertaking totalled 4¹/₂ route miles, and at the time was isolated from the rest of the S.L.T. system, though connected at Moses Gate with the Bolton Corporation tramways. Farnworth was at that time a fairly compact town of 26,000 inhabitants, while Kearsley had just under 10,000, more widely scattered.

Farnworth Horse Tramway

The Farnworth tramways were all older than those of the S.L.T. The first tramway in the town ran along the main Bolton to Manchester road (Bolton Road and Market Street) from the town's northern boundary at Moses Gate to its southern boundary at the corner of Longcauseway, just beyond the *Black Horse* Inn. This line, opened on Friday, 3rd June 1881, formed part of the standard-gauge horse tramway system based on Bolton Horse-drawn trams had already started to run the two miles from Bolton to Moses Gate on Wednesday, 1st September 1880. The Bolton tramway system was promoted jointly by the Borough of Bolton and the Local Boards of Astley Bridge (absorbed by Bolton in 1898), Farnworth, and Kearsley, and was authorised by the Bolton and Suburban Tramways Order, 1878, confirmed on 16th August 1878 by the Tramways Orders Confirmation (No. 2) Act (41 & 42 Vic., cap. ccxxxi). Although the whole system was leased for operating purposes to Messrs. Edmund Holden and Company, each of the local authorities concerned was responsible for construction and maintenance in its own district. Bolton Corporation was responsible for those sections which lay entirely outside the areas of any of the owning authorities. On the Farnworth line, the length of about one mile from Burnden to Moses Gate came into this category, for it lay in the township of Great Lever, which was not absorbed by Bolton until 1898. Unbelievable as it may seem today, this length from Burnden to Moses Gate was then entirely rural. The whole line from Bolton to Farnworth was double track. From Moses Gate onwards it lay entirely in Farnworth for a distance of 63¹/₂ chains, but for 10¹/₂ chains from Church Lane (later re-named Church Road, and not to be confused with Church Street, some 200 yards further north), the track on the west side of the street lay in Farnworth, and the other track in Kearsley. Finally, for the last five chains, both tracks were in Kearsley.

Some explanation of local geography is necessary here. Though the main street past the *Black Horse* is one end of Farnworth's main street (Market Street) and really forms the natural town centre of the built-up area formed by Farnworth and the more densely populated part of Kearsley, the east side of it, including the *Black Horse*, is actually in Kearsley for some 250 yards. For this section, the Farnworth side of the street is known as Manchester Road, and the Kearsley side as Higher Market Street. The road junction with Longcauseway, at the south end of Higher Market Street, however, is entirely in Kearsley, owing to the curvature of the street and the boundary in opposite directions. Transport undertakings have usually seemed to regard the *Black Horse* as being in Farnworth; for many years now buses terminating at or near this point have displayed the destination "Farnworth (*Black Horse*)", and in this form it also appears in the timetables. S. L. T. trams also displayed this destination, but Bolton Corporation trams always displayed merely *Black Horse*, while Farnworth Council, in the days of independent operation, referred to it as "Kearsley". The horse trams had the destination "Farnworth" painted on the side.

At the horse tram terminus, the double track continued to a dead end immediately beyond a turning circle, for it was authorised to continue a further 1¹/₂ miles along Bolton Road and Manchester Road to the Kearsley/Clifton boundary at Unity Brook. Another line was authorised to run westwards along Longcauseway, and then north along Albert Road, finally turning east along Gladstone Road to rejoin the Moses Gate-Black Horse line at the east end of Gladstone Road. This line, unlike the other, was to be single-track, and would have had only one passing loop in its 1¹/₄ miles. In fact, neither of these lines was constructed during the horse tram era. The turning circle at the terminus was in fact not used, and was disconnected at an early date, for the cars normally used on the Farnworth service were of Eade's patent reversible type, in which the body could swivel right round on the chassis, thus dispensing with the necessity of unharnessing the horse at a dead-end terminus, and also permitting a single-ended body with only one staircase.

A further Bolton and Suburban Tramways Order, confirmed on 24th July 1888 by the Tramways Orders Confirmation (No.2) Act (51 & 52 Vict., cap. xcv) authorised the introduction of steam, cable, or electric traction, on the Bolton horse tram routes - many of them being steeply graded, some form of mechanical traction was an attractive proposition - but in fact these powers were not exercised. By the Bolton Corporation Tramways Act of 9th June 1893 (56 & 57 Vict.,cap. lv), Bolton Corporation was authorised to work the tramways, including the lines in Farnworth and Kearsley, if it was

unable to lease them at an adequate rent. Finally, the Bolton Tramways and Improvements Act of 15th July 1897 (60 & 61 Vict., cap. cxxxiv), in addition to authorising various new tramways - none of them in the Farnworth area - authorised the Corporation to electrify the Bolton and Suburban tramways, and work them itself, whether or not it was possible to find a lessee. Following this Act, Messrs. Holden agreed in June 1899 to surrender their lease although it still had three years to run. They received £58,000 in compensation, but continued to operate horse tram services on a temporary basis until electrification work was completed.

Electrification

The first electric tram routes in Bolton were opened on Saturday, 9th December 1899, and the last horse trams ran on Monday, 1st January 1900. Moses Gate was among the routes worked electrically from 2nd January, but electrification work in Farnworth had only begun in December and was as yet nothing like complete. As a result, Farnworth was left without any service at all. The Urban District Council protested to Bolton Corporation and asked for a horse tram service between Moses Gate and *Black Horse*, but the Corporation replied that it did not possess any horse trams, and that if it were to buy one or two from Messrs. Holden, it would have nowhere to keep the horses. However, Farnworth U.D.C. managed to persuade Holden's to provide a temporary horse bus service.

By the end of March the electrification of the Farnworth section was complete, though not the short length to Kearsley. As in Bolton, the track was not relaid, but merely had the joints bonded. As there was then no electricity supply in Farnworth, the overhead wires were fed from the Bolton distribution system. A trial trip was made as far as Church Lane on the afternoon of Tuesday, 27th March 1900; the local newspaper commented that this trip occasioned great interest; "the car made a great noise in its passage ... The news soon got about, and the return journey was made though the midst of a great throng."

The official inspection took place a few days later, by which time the Kearsley section was also ready, but no service began, as Bolton was short of trams. Farnworth U.D.C. asked for the line to be opened in time for the Easter holidays, but Bolton replied that it was hoped to open the Horwich extension then, and there were insufficient cars to open Farnworth as well. However, some last-minute difficulties arose in connection with the Horwich line, and so the electric tram service to the *Black Horse* began on Good Friday, 13th April 1900, without any previous notice. Workmen had spent most of the previous night cleaning dirt and stones out of the rail grooves.

Farnworth U.D.C. Act, 1900.

Farnworth U.D.C. had already decided to extend the tramway system. Originally they had hoped to enter into partnership with Kearsley U.D.C., to form a joint electric lighting and tramway undertaking, but were advised that this would not be legal, and they therefore proceeded independently. After obtaining an Electric Lighting Order, they began to consider the problem of tramways. After unsuccessful negotiations with Bolton Corporation, it was decided not only to construct additional tramways but to work them independently, and on 13th December 1899 the decision was taken to promote a Parliamentary Bill for various purposes: part I was concerned with tramways. This duly became the Farnworth Urban District Council Act on 6th August 1900 (63 & 64 Vict., cap. ccxxxiii). The Act authorised the construction of 5 miles 56 chains of tramway - quite a considerable amount for a fairly compact town of its size. 4 miles 19 chains were to be double track: the Council did not, of course, really think the town was extensive or populous enough to support a self-contained system of such a size, with so high a proportion of double track, but so many other tramways were now being proposed in surrounding districts that it seemed that the Farnworth tramways would become a vital link in a large network, with the Council participating in several profitable and important through services. Their main hopes centred on the town's position astride the Bolton-Manchester road, but heavy traffic was expected in other directions too. It was the

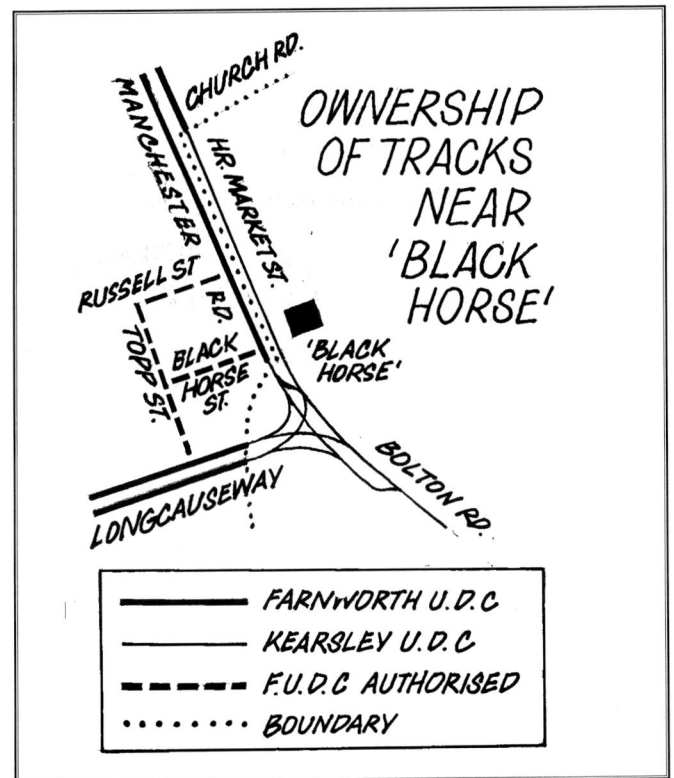

OWNERSHIP OF TRACKS NEAR 'BLACK HORSE'

———————— FARNWORTH U.D.C

———————— KEARSLEY U.D.C

– – – – – – F.U.D.C AUTHORISED

· · · · · · · · BOUNDARY

Plate 23, below. On 1st April 1906 the South Lancashire Tramways Company took over the tramways of Farnworth Urban District Council. Some years earlier, Farnworth had seen itself as an important link in the proposed tramway network, and, in expectation of considerable profits, had chosen to operate its own independent tramway. This was the scene at the Farnworth/Bolton boundary at Moses Gate in May 1901 as re-construction of the former horse-drawn tramway began.

Plate 36. Car No.72 passes the new entrance to Worsley New Hall as it rounds the curve at Worsley Court House on the Swinton-Atherton service.

H.Grundy, commercial postcard.

Gauge conversion in Hindley.

In the Autumn of 1906, the S.L.T. at last carried out the conversion to standard-gauge, and electrification, of the Market Street line at Hindley, disused since 1904. The various extensions authorised in Hindley were not built. The reconstructed Market Street line was connected only to the S.L.T. tracks and not to the Wigan Road tracks operated by Wigan, and remained without a service for another 21 years.

Christmas Snowstorm.

What was probably the heaviest snowstorm during the tramway period occurred on the evening of Christmas Day 1906. Some 20 or 30 cars had to be abandoned on the road. On Wednesday 26th December, it took all day to get the abandoned cars from east of Tyldesley as far as Hindsford. The Leigh-Atherton section was re-opened on 27th December, and Leigh-Lowton on the 28th, but several more days elapsed before all lines were again in operation.

Plate 37. Problems of maintenance in the war years followed by post-war inflation, meant that the transport industry passed through a difficult period in the early 1920s. Car No.59, still bearing the original short top-cover, looks somewhat neglected as it stops at the bottom end of Bolton Road, Walkden, on the Moses Gate service.

Clifton Light Railway.

A further extension, 1 mile 32 chains in length (of which 25 chains were double track) from the existing terminus on the Kearsley boundary at Unity Brook, through Clifton to the Pendlebury boundary at the *Oddfellows' Arms*, Newtown, was opened on Thursday, 28th February 1907. This line had been authorised by a Light Railway Order confirmed on 21st December 1901, granted to Barton-upon-Irwell Rural District Council. Clifton parish was a detached part of this Rural District. The Council had tried in 1901 to persuade Salford Corporation to construct the line, known as the "Clifton Light Railway". Now, at last, the S.L.T. agreed to construct the line and to maintain and operate it, though it would be the property of the Rural District Council. Construction work had begun in November 1906. The Moses Gate to "Clifton" (i.e. Unity Brook) service was extended over the new line, running every fifteen minutes for most of the day. The destination was still shown as "Clifton" on the cars, though more usually referred to as "Newtown" in the timetables. There was a gap of 200 yards between the terminus of the Clifton Light Railway at the *Oddfellows' Arms*, and the nearest point reached by Salford trams, the *Windmill Hotel*, Pendlebury (tracks owned by Swinton & Pendlebury U.D.C.).

Negotiations were opened with Salford Corporation with a view to closing the gap, but with no success, and in fact it was not until twenty years later that a connection was constructed.

The Winton Branch.

The length of line between Worsley Court House and Winton *(Brown Cow)* remained unused for some six months, but opened for traffic on Good Friday 29th March 1907. Salford cars worked only as far as Winton, and the scheme to link with S.L.T. cars at the Alder Forest boundary had not materialised. However, at Easter 1907, Salford, without reference to Eccles Council, whose lines it leased, gave permission for S.L.T cars on the Atherton-Swinton service to divert to serve Winton over the Eccles tracks, there to connect with Salford cars on the Manchester (Deansgate) to Peel Green services. The long Atherton-Moses Gate service thereby being split, S.L.T cars on the Moses Gate-Swinton section meanwhile continued to Worsley, a popular destination at holiday periods. It was evident that this arrangement was satisfactory to both operators, but not to Eccles councillors, who argued that Salford had no right to sub-let the lease. The result was that S.L.T. cars were barred from the Eccles tracks on the Alder Forest-Winton section. Salford did not choose to work over the S.L.T. section to Worsley, so the Worsley-Winton length was left without a service of any sort. The withdrawal of trams did

not please the residents along the route who petitioned the Board of Trade to compel one or other of the parties to commence a regular service. The Board of Trade responded that it had no powers to do as requested.

Excursions and Outings.

At that time, of course, when people did not travel far from home for a day's outing, Worsley was a much-favoured local beauty spot. The rearrangement of services over the 1907 Easter holidays was intended to cater for this traffic. A further encouragement to "tourist" traffic from Bolton was a special 9d ticket introduced about this time, and valid either as a return ticket from Four Lane Ends to Worsley via Atherton, or as a single ticket from Four Lane Ends to Moses Gate via Atherton, Worsley, and Swinton, with break of journey at Worsley.

Even the S.L.T. employees and their families had an outing by tram at least twice about this period. On Tuesday, 14th August 1906, and again on Wednesday 28th August 1907, they were all invited to Knowsley Park by the Hon. Arthur Stanley. A meal was provided and sports and similar events organised. On each occasion special cars ran through from Atherton to Prescot. On the first occasion at least one car ran through from Farnworth, via Bolton; the following year, Swinton depot having replaced Farnworth, there were two cars from Swinton, via Boothstown - a 25-mile journey. A similar outing probably took place in later years but no details are known.

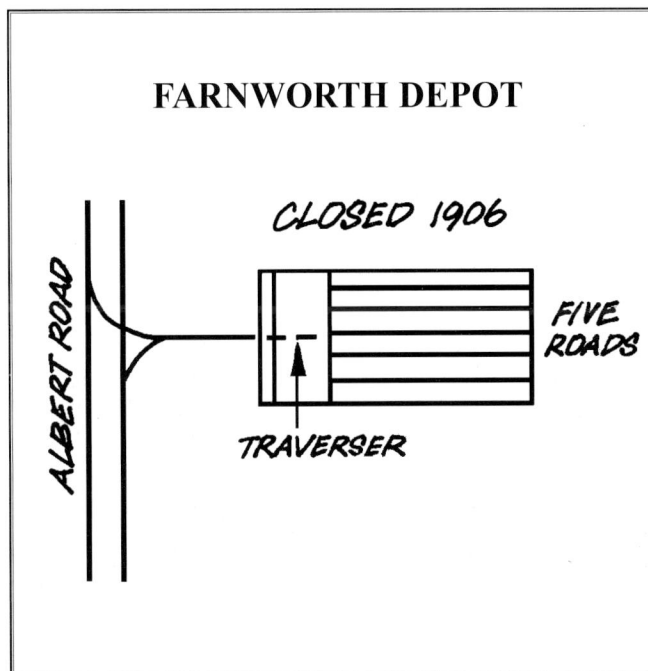

FARNWORTH DEPOT

CLOSED 1906

ALBERT ROAD

FIVE ROADS

TRAVERSER

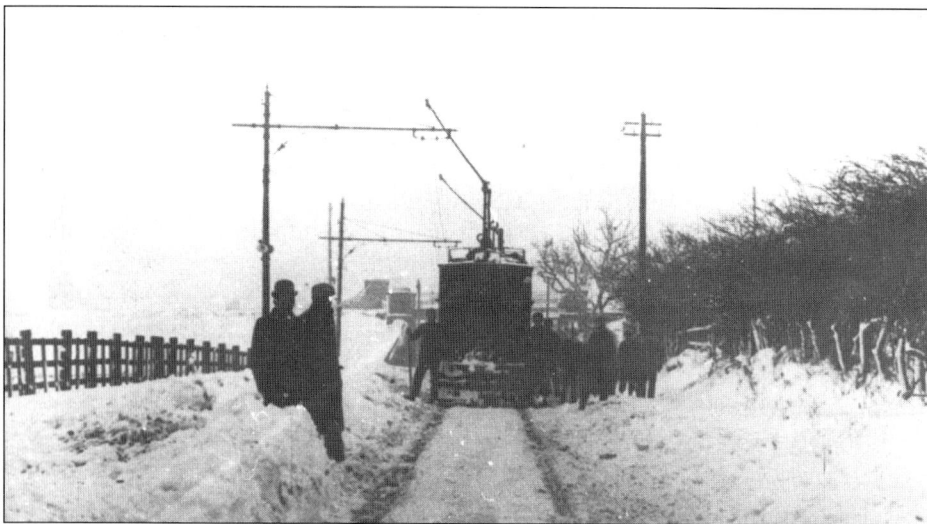

Plate 38. Christmas time 1906 saw an unusually heavy snowfall, leading to the abandonment of several tramcars. The leading snowplough appears to be the water car, whilst an open-top car stands behind. Staff were hard at work rescuing stranded trams and attempting to keep the lines clear.

Plate 39. CarNo.27 was called in to assist the snowplough by running up and down the cleared lines to prevent further build-up of obstructions.

Plate 40. Covered top car No.69 was also involved in snow clearance. Seen near Four Lane Ends, its destination reads LOWTON ST. MARY'S.

Plate 41. Pending the construction of the SLT lines between Walkden and Farnworth, an independent horse-drawn omnibus service operated from a terminus in front of the *Stocks Hotel,* Walkden. This service connected with the Farnworth tramway route to Moses Gate at the Brookhouse boundary. There were complaints that tram drivers started off as soon as the omnibus came into view.

Plate 42. At the time of the 1906 take-over, the Farnworth system remained detached from the other SLT lines, but work started immediately on the construction of track from Farnworth (Brookhouse) to Walkden, to which point the line from Swinton would eventually come. SLT operated the Farnworth Cars from the Albert Road depot, and passenger services from Moses Gate via Brookhouse to Walkden began immediately after track inspection on the 29th June 1906. This postcard view claims to show the first passenger car from Walkden on June 30th, the first full day of operation.

Commercial postcard.

Plate 43. Farnworth cars Nos 2 and 9 at Walkden on the first full day of operation, Saturday 30th June 1906. Car No.9, at the rear, had been hired by the Walkden Wesley Guild for a special trip to Horwich, which would have meant an excursion into Bolton territory, assuming that passengers were not forced to change cars at Moses Gate. Note that car No.2 has the original glass destination screen, whilst car No.9, of the later batch, has a roller blind.

The last extension - Little Hulton

Work on the S.L.T. line between Walkden Memorial and Farnworth via Little Hulton was begun in March 1913, but the length from Cleggs Lane corner to Greenheys (Bolton boundary) also re-authorised by the 1911 Act, was not constructed. Most of the new line lay in Little Hulton Urban District (later absorbed by Worsley) which had long pressed for the line to be built and was persuaded to be responsible for its maintenance though it did not own it! The Council soon discovered that it had made a bad bargain.

The 44 chains in Farnworth, along Buckley Lane from the boundary to the junction with Albert Road and Longcauseway, where the points had been laid complete in 1901, was the property of Farnworth U.D.C., and brought Farnworth's total route mileage up to 3 miles 18 chains.* The mileage owned by the S.L.T. was now 32 miles 40 chains, of which 9 miles 74 chains were double track.

*Some years later the mileage was returned as 3 miles exactly; this can only be accounted for by the removal of the connecting curves at Moses Gate and by ceasing to count the length near Black Horse where only one track was owned by Farnworth. There is no obvious explanation of why the mileage was returned in 1920-23 as only 2 miles 68 chains.

The new line was inspected on Friday 22nd August 1913, but permission to open was refused, principally because the L. & N.W. Railway Company objected that the bridge over the railway in Cleggs Lane did not comply with Board of Trade Regulations, and that the bridge in Manchester Road, at Little Hulton Station, was too weak for tram traffic. Mr. Edwardes protested that ever since construction work had begun, he had been trying without success to obtain plans of the Cleggs Lane bridge from the railway company in order to decide what alterations were necessary. He also pointed out that the Manchester Road bridge was crossed innumerable times every day by traction engines and "lurries" far heavier than any tram. A celebratory luncheon, already arranged, was held despite "this great disappointment". In the speeches, the Railway company was strongly criticised while the S.L.T. was praised for the benefits it had brought to the district.

A few days later, permission was granted to cross the Manchester Road bridge, and the line was opened to traffic on Thursday, 28th August. For the time being, passengers had to alight at the Cleggs Lane bridge and cross on foot to join a connecting car waiting on the other side. Cars were first allowed over the bridge on Saturday, 6th September. The service between Walkden and *Black*

Plate 45. The district of Little Hulton gained a tramway in 1913 when tracks were completed along Manchester Road and Cleggs Lane to offer an alternative route between Walkden and Farnworth. The official party is seen alongside the special car. This side view of the car illustrates the distinctive livery and elaborate gilt lining-out on the panels, which by this date was being seen by the manager as an unnecessary expense. The bracing rods for the top-deck cover may also be noted.   *Harrison, Walkden.*

Plate 46. The car used for the official inspection of the Little Hulton lines on Friday 22nd August 1913 was either number 59 or 69 one of the 1906 batch of top-covered cars. Subsequently, there were complaints that only open top cars were used on the Little Hulton services, to which SLT replied that these were the only cars available. *Harrison, Walkden.*

Horse via Little Hulton operated every twenty minutes, and restored daily service along Longcauseway for the first time in eight years. In November, transfer tickets were introduced between Little Hulton and Moses Gate (ld.) and Little Hulton and Wardley (ld.),though at first the transfer tickets were issued only in one direction; from Little Hulton.

There were complaints about the use only of open-top cars on this line, but the S.L.T. replied that these were the only cars available. Some cars were in a very poor state of repair, and Worsley Council reported to the Board of Trade that some were in dangerous condition.

The S.L.T. was always remarkably free from serious accidents, and indeed had a very good record for a system consisting mainly of single-track. There were, of course, collisions with other road vehicles from time to time, and occasional cases of pedestrians being knocked down, sometimes with fatal results, but what might be described as "tram accidents" pure and simple were almost unknown. About this time, however, there were two accidents which could easily have been far more serious than was actually the case. Early in the morning of Wednesday, 23rd April 1913, a car from Four Lane Ends got out of control descending Firs Brow, in Newbrook Road and ran through a loop without stopping. Another car was ascending from Atherton, but a collision was avoided by the quick thinking of the driver of this latter car, who reversed down the hill when he realised that the descending car was out of control. Unfortunately some of the passengers on the ascending car became alarmed

when it reversed and collision seemed imminent, and scrambling to the rear platform, they jumped off. The conductor was knocked off the car in the rush, and received injuries from which he died. A year later, two cars collided head-on in Buckley Lane in thick fog, but although both cars were badly damaged, there were no serious injuries.

At the opening of the Little Hulton line, Mr. Edwardes had expressed strong opinions about unnecessary decoration on cars. Although the financial situation of the undertaking was slowly improving, no dividend had yet been paid on ordinary shares, and there had even been difficulty in making the dividend payments on the 5% preference shares. Strict economy was necessary. At the Tramways and Light Railway Association conference earlier in 1913, Mr. Edwardes had also mentioned this point. In his opinion far too much money was spent on elaborate gilt lining-out and polished brass handrails; over a period of time these represented considerable expenditure. "Absolutely plain painting" was the best; similarly, some undertakings spent far too much on elaborate uniforms for the crews. Neat uniforms there must be - but not with elaborate piping and trimmings. Few economies were possible in track maintenance, for constantly increasing road traffic was increasing the wear on tramway tracks and paving; but economy in both construction and maintenance could be made by omitting elaborate scrollwork and fluted pole bases (which were merely traps for hidden corrosion) from the poles: this policy was followed on the Little Hulton extension.

More freight traffic proposals

The goods traffic proposal was again revived in 1913. There was enthusiastic support from most of the undertakings involved. Liverpool Corporation and the S.L.T. were the keenest supporters. Mr. Edwardes announced that negotiations were in progress for carrying coal from a mineral railway to a proposed coal yard, a distance of five miles - unfortunately it has not been possible to trace where on the S.L.T. system this was to be. Owing to the impossibility of running railway wagons on standard-gauge tram track with its narrow grooves, it was intended to use transporter-trucks; unfortunately the fact that the gauges were the same made it difficult to design a transporter with a sufficiently low centre of gravity. On a narrow-gauge tramway it would have been easier, as the wheels of the railway wagons would have been well outside the ends of the axles of the transporter. Unfortunately nothing came of this scheme. While the negotiations were going on, plans for goods traffic all over South Lancashire were again being discussed. Mr. C. W. Mallins, the General Manager of Liverpool Corporation Tramways investigated the matter thoroughly for his Committee - for without the support of Liverpool no goods scheme could be successful - and supported it strongly. It was intended this time to run three-car trains, and it was said that provisional consent had been obtained from the Board of Trade. The trains would have a carrying capacity of 25 tons. It was calculated that 288 trains per day could be handled via Knotty Ash, with the heaviest traffic at night; 36 motor cars and 72 wagons would be necessary. But until considerable track doubling had been carried out on the S.L.T. system, the S.L.T. would only be able to handle much less than this. The S.L.T. would be prepared to double much of its track if a small-scale experiment proved successful for which it was suggested that 14 motor cars and 28 trailers would be adequate, provided partly by Liverpool and partly by the S.L.T. Much thought had been given to the question of constructing sidings into mills and factories: this could only be justified if there was to be a guaranteed heavy traffic to any one place. It would probably be better to construct goods yards and use motor vehicles for local delivery. Overall journey times from Liverpool Docks would still be less than by rail, and much less than by ordinary road transport. All-night traffic would be economical to run as the power stations would have the advantage of a heavy traction load throughout 24 hours. It was felt that if the scheme were to be successful, the goods traffic could not be handled on the existing Liverpool Corporation tracks. Recommended were new tramways in Liverpool along the whole line of docks parallel to the dock railway which ran beneath the Overhead Railway, and two new routes to Knotty Ash from the North and South docks respectively, with a marshalling yard and sorting sidings at Knotty Ash. The northern route would be by way of Walton Village and West Derby, the southern via Mill Street, Earle Road, and Rathbone Road to Old Swan. There were also suggestions that the goods traffic might be better handled by trolley vehicles; the cost of installing additional overhead wires would be less than the cost of additional track construction, though the permissible loads would be less. Trolley vehicles also fitted with batteries, similar to the trolley-lorry then in use in Bradford, would be able to carry goods directly to and from factories off the tram routes.

The Mersey Docks and Harbour Board was opposed to the whole scheme, principally because of track complications in the Dock area. Nevertheless, this scheme was much more carefully investigated than the 1903 one, and it is quite probable that had war not broken out, goods traffic would eventually have begun, and the whole history of tramways in South Lancashire might have been very different.

Another scheme stopped by the outbreak of war was a through tram service between Bolton and Manchester. After discussions between Bolton and Salford Corporations and the S. L. T. in May 1914, Salford agreed to construct the necessary 200-yard connection at Pendlebury, from the Windmill Hotel to the S.L.T. terminus at Newtown ("Clifton"), but before work could begin, war broke out.

SWINTON DEPOT

PARTINGTON LANE

SEVEN ROAD TRAM SHED

War effort

The outbreak of war in August 1914 caused several reductions in services, though it was some time before they were seriously affected. The trams remained very busy, and indeed traffic began to increase steadily, for there was a severe reduction in train services, particularly on certain lines which closely parallelled tram routes, such as Kenyon Junction to Bolton, and large numbers of people changed jobs so that workpeople's traffic also increased.

In May, Lancashire United had purchased three Dennis charabancs with the object of finding out how they would stand up to the roads of the area, and all three were requisitioned. This did not have any serious effect, as they had been used only on excursions and for private parties, and no bus services had yet been started with these vehicles.

Most of the S.L.T.'s workshop accommodation was turned over to the manufacture of shells, and for a considerable period production was 1,000 per week. Nearly all the office and maintenance staff, from General Manager downwards, spent part of their working time on this job. Eventually, of course, this diversion of labour and equipment began to have a serious effect on tramcar maintenance.

However, the hitherto unused tram depot at Platt Bridge was brought into use in 1914, when the fitting of top covers to some of the Milnes cars was carried out there. In 1916 the depot saw further use for a time, when the track was cut during the rebuilding of the Great Central Railway bridge at Hindley and Platt Bridge (formerly Strangeways and Hindley, later Hindley South) station.

While this work was in progress, six cars were stabled at Platt Bridge to operate the service between there and Ashton.

Bolton Corporation had been steadily doubling the track on the Four Lane Ends route. Daubhill to Hulton Lane had been doubled in 1910 and Hulton Lane to Plodder Lane in 1913. Now, in 1915, the last 200 yards from Plodder Lane to Four Lane Ends were doubled, and this involved re-aligning the last 25 yards of S.L.T. track, for which the S.L.T. provided the materials, while Bolton carried out the work.

Through cars to Bolton suspended

For three days commencing Saturday 22nd May 1915, the Bolton tramwaymen were on strike, and S.L.T. cars turned back at the boundaries.

Towards the end of 1915, the Company, like most other undertakings, was badly affected by shortage of staff, over 30 percent having joined the Armed Forces. It was no longer possible to avoid engaging "female guards" (the Company always followed the Manchester practice of describing its conductors as "Guards"), though this step was taken reluctantly. Rather to its surprise, the Company found that it had no reason to be dissatisfied with the "female guards". The through service between Lowton and Bolton was discontinued with effect from Monday 13th December 1915, and once again all passengers had to change at Four Lane Ends. From the same date, the Bolton to Clifton service was curtailed to *Black Horse*, and the *Black Horse* to Clifton section became linked operationally with the service from Walkden to *Black Horse* via Little Hulton.

The impression was allowed to prevail that these curtailments were the result of objections by Bolton Corporation to the use of Conductresses, but in fact Bolton also began to employ women a couple of weeks after this.

Plate 47. Car No.10 in the mid-1920s on the Kearsley U.D.C. tracks between Farnworth *(Black Horse)* and Clifton. Not often on the S.L.T. system did one see centre poles supporting the overhead wires.
Charles Wilkinson.

Wigan problems

In January 1914, Wigan had definitely resolved to lay in a connection at Hindley to enable through running, but once again nothing had been done. However, Hindley U.D.C. were becoming more and more concerned about the derelict Market Street line, and in January 1915 suggested that Wigan should take it over. It would seem that the S.L.T was quite agreeable, as there was no convenient way in which it could be fitted into their arrangement of services, but Hindley spoiled its case by trying to insist that Wigan should build an extension from the top of Market Street in the Westhoughton direction as far as the Hindley boundary, about ¾ mile. Neither the S.L.T. nor Wigan Corporation wanted this.

Late in 1915, after a meeting with Wigan Tramways Committee, Mr. Edwardes promised to recommend to his Board that Wigan Corporation should operate Market Street and pay £25 per annum to the S.L.T.: the S.L.T. to supply current and street lighting, Wigan to maintain the track and overhead. About the same time, it was reported that Hindley U.D.C. had agreed to lower the roadway under the Lancashire Union Railway bridge in Wigan Road, to enable double-deck cars to run to Hindley. Wigan had purchased some top-covered double-deck standard-gauge cars in 1914. Finally, Wigan agreed to take over the Market Street line and to apply at the earliest opportunity for powers to extend along Castle Hill Road as far as the Hindley/Westhoughton boundary - but once again all these plans came to nothing.

Between November 1915 and March 1916 the Wigan Corporation system was seriously affected by repeated breakdowns at the power station, and S.L.T. supplied current to Wigan's Platt Bridge route by an emergency connection at Platt Bridge. As a result, this route was kept going without interruption (though there must have been a considerable voltage drop towards Wigan) and on some occasions it was the only Wigan route operating. For instance, all Wigan tramways except Platt Bridge were closed completely from 22nd to 25th January 1916 inclusive and there were other similar stoppages of several hours' duration, as well as innumerable occasions when only parts of the Wigan system could be kept going. The S.L.T. ceased to supply current on 24th March, but Wigan's problems were not over, for occasional stoppages occurred until the autumn. When it came to paying the bill, Wigan Tramways Committee was surprised and delighted to find that it had to pay the S.L.T. only four-fifths of what it would have paid its own Corporation's Electricity Department for the same amount of current.

More new traffic

A new form of traffic came to the S.L.T. in 1916: prisoners of war. Large numbers of German prisoners were carried daily under armed guard from their "camp" (actually a disused factory) at Leigh to various places in the district where they were working: the principal destinations were Chanters Colliery, between Atherton and Tyldesley, and Lowton St. Mary's station, for trains to Irlam. Some reports claim that for this traffic a few cars - possibly cars which had been "cannibalised" to keep others running during the wartime shortage of spares -were used as trailer cars, but this cannot definitely be confirmed: the problem is discussed further in chapter six.

Even local newspapers were more occupied with other events in the years 1914 to 1918, and little is recorded of tramway happenings, but in any event there are few changes to record during the war and for a few years after. Like many systems, the S.L.T. emerged from the war years in a sorry state of repair, and the end of the war brought no immediate end to the war-time shortage of materials. Indeed, it can safely be said that neither cars nor permanent way ever fully recovered from their enforced war-time neglect, though a determined effort was made to improve the cars by fitting new trucks, new top-covers, and in some cases virtually new bodies.

On the credit side, traffic was now 75% above the pre-war level, with a slight decrease in traffic mileage: the number of passenger journeys rose from nearly 14 million in 1913 to 19½ million in 1917, and nearly 26 million in 1919. This increase of traffic led to the first payment of dividend on Ordinary Shares.

Increases of costs during the war had led to increases in fares, for although the increase in traffic had absorbed some of the quickly rising costs, it could not do so entirely. Certain fares were increased on Monday 24th December, 1917, but this could only be done within the maximum of 1d. per mile laid down by the 1900 Act. To overcome this difficulty, common to many undertakings, Parliament passed in 1918 the Statutory Undertakings (Temporary Increase of Charges) Act, and under this Act the S.L.T. was authorised by an Order of 15th December 1919 to make further increases. With a few exceptions, fares from 1d.. to 2½d. were increased by ½d. and higher fares by 1d. The 1d. fare was not abolished but now covered a shorter distance. Examples of the new fares are Atherton to Ashton 7d., Atherton to Swinton 7d., Lowton St. Mary's to Four Lane Ends 7d., Swinton to Moses Gate 5d., *Black Horse* to Newtown 4d., Walkden to *Black Horse* via Little Hulton 3d. Workmen's return fares were ½d or 1d. above the corresponding single fares. Under the provisions of the Tramways (Temporary Increase of Charges) Act 1920, the operation of the original Order was extended from time to time, not always without opposition from local authorities. However, there was no further increase in ordinary fares until 1951: a remarkable period of stability. Indeed, the introduction of a number of return fares in the thirties led to cheaper travel for some passengers.

St. Helens undertaking Municipalised

St. Helens Corporation refused to renew the lease of its system when it expired, and took over operation itself on 1st October 1919, purchasing the 36 cars of the New St. Helens and District Tramways Company, which was put into liquidation. This made no difference to the arrangements for the working of the Haydock-Ashton section. As the loss of the St. Helens system isolated the Liverpool & Prescot line from the other tramways in the L.U.T. Group, arrangements were made to sell that line to Liverpool Corporation with effect from the same date. The L.L.R. Company was also put into liquidation, and its seven cars were transferred to the S.L.T.

Development of motor-bus services

The main effort of the L.U.T. Group in the post-war period was directed to the development of motor-bus services. Although this book is not concerned with this form of transport, it is necessary to outline briefly the development of services, which were soon to have an effect on the future of the tramways. All these bus services were operated by Lancashire United, not by the S.L.T. itself, but the two companies were administered to all intents and purposes as one undertaking, though naturally the accounts were kept separate.

The L.U.T. re-entered the motor-bus business, after its abortive attempt in 1914, with vehicles purchased from the War Department in 1919. By 12th September the Company had twenty-two 40 h.p. Dennis 28-seaters, and one pneumatic-tyred 24 h.p. Unic 14-seater. Twenty-eight Dennis and five Unic buses were on order. For some months only private hire and excursion business was handled, but a regular bus service between Lowton St. Mary's, Newton-le-Willows, and Earlestown was introduced on Friday 18th June 1920. The first new motor-buses - three A.E.C. 45/50 h.p. 35-seaters - were delivered in October, and by then services were also operating from Lowton St. Mary's to Golborne, and from Golborne via Newton-le-Willows and Winwick to the Warrington Corporation tram terminus at Longford. From then on, development was rapid, and services soon became more than feeders to tram routes. However, there was some competition: Leigh Corporation, under powers granted by its Act of 4th August 1920 (10 & 11 Geo.V., cap.lxxvii) began on Tuesday 9th November 1920 to operate buses from Plank Lane to the Cemetery and from Leigh to Tamar, and shortly afterwards the Cemetery route was extended to Astley: the Corporation was prohibited from operating along the tram route in the borough without the consent of the S.L.T.

By 1925, the L.U.T. had almost 100 buses, and the 21 services covered most of the roads served to-day (except of course for housing developments and new roads built since that time), but no buses ran along tram routes for anything but a short distance, and most services did not begin until mid-day. At first, too, the company could not gain access to towns such as Bolton, Salford, and St. Helens, which were operating tramways. Wigan, after initial misgivings, was more co-operative and issued licences for L.U.T. services into Wigan, subject to a protective fare. The L.U.T. acquired its first double-deck buses in 1927, and by 1929, when it owned 152 vehicles, all the principal services were similar to to-day: agreements for joint operation and through running, defining areas of operation, such as the agreement of 15th June 1928 with Leigh Corporation, had been reached with most of the surrounding municipalities and with Ribble Motor Services Ltd., of Preston. The buses and services of Trafford Park Estates Ltd., had been purchased in 1925. It was therefore possible to develop a dense network of

Plate 48, Worsley UDC had complained that some of the cars were in poor condition, and, perhaps reacting to criticism, in 1914-15 the Company began a programme of improvements by purchasing 25 top-covers to be fitted to some of the first 45 open cars. Car No.8, seen here during the First World War with conductress, received such a cover. Unlike the short covers on the 59-82 series, the roofs, whilst retaining open ends, were extended to provide protection over the stair top.

Plate 53. A new Walkden to Manchester service, operated jointly with Salford, began in 1926. Salford allocated the service number 61 to the new joint route, but it is doubtful if this was ever displayed. Passengers joining at intermediate stops had to re-book at Swinton Church, terminus of Salford's Swinton route, and close to the S.L.T. Depot in nearby Partington Lane. S.L.T. conductor Gilbert Elliott, carrying ticket rack and cash bag, leaves his tram standing alongside Salford car No.287 as crews change duty in 1930.

Plate 54. Joint services with Salford into Manchester were proposed in 1925-26. Only a few yards of track connection were required. Swinton Council raised objections as it had done in earlier years, on the grounds that changes might reduce the service frequency along Station Road. Nevertheless, connection was made first at Swinton Church. The joint service was to be operated on a proportional mileage basis, using five Salford and three S.L.T. cars. In accordance with Salford's policy, the S.L.T. vehicles would not display any external advertising. The cars selected were three of the ex-Farnworth 86-seat bogies (Nos.46, 53 & 57) together with the two new cars (44 & 45), plus one small car (No.42) kept in reserve in case of breakdown. Car No.44 is in Bridge Street, Manchester, approaching Deansgate, carrying Salford type route boards on the upper deck panels. The rear destination has already been turned to show WALKDEN. *W.Gratwicke.*

Tram services in 1925

The operating day had been shortened during the war, and neither the pre-war hours nor the pre-war frequency were ever fully restored. Even more severe cuts had been necessary for a time in 1921 during a coal shortage, and a similar shortage was still having some effects in 1925. In general, services started about 5.00 a.m. though one or two longer services had outward departures from about 4.30 in order to provide reasonable return services, and the last cars were generally back in the depots about 11.30 p.m. on Mondays to Fridays, and just after midnight on Saturdays.

The Lowton to Four Lane Ends service, still the busiest, provided a ten-minute frequency throughout the day between Leigh Market and Four Lane Ends, with alternate cars extended to and from Lowton St. Mary's. The first through car from Lowton was not until 5.35 a.m. On Saturdays from noon, all cars ran to and from Lowton, and the last through cars were 10.25p.m. from Lowton and 10.30 from Four Lane Ends: ten minutes later than on Mondays to Fridays.

Between Atherton and Ashton a twenty-minute service was provided throughout the day, starting with the 4.50 a.m. and ending with the 9.30 p.m. from Atherton. On Saturdays, the interval was reduced to 15 minutes from midday, and the last cars were 45 minutes later: there was also an early 'workmen's car' on Saturdays, from Atherton at 4.00 a.m. and Ashton at 5.00. From 1 .00 p.m. on Saturdays all cars ran through to and from Leigh.

The Atherton to Swinton section was noticeably less frequent than before 1914: the first cars in 1925 left Atherton at 5.30 a.m. and Swinton at 6.00 a.m., and only a half-hourly service was provided until about noon, after which a twenty-minute service operated until the last through cars at 10.30 p.m. from Atherton and 11.10 p.m. from Swinton: the latter would not reach Atherton depot until after midnight, and was the only car running so late on Mondays to Fridays. On Saturdays the services started half an hour later but finished at the same time, and the twenty-minute service started at 10.30 a.m. From 5.45 to 9.15 a.m. and from noon to close of service, the frequency was doubled daily (except Sunday morning) by a shuttle service between Atherton and Boothstown, and on Saturdays these Boothstown cars ran through to and from Leigh after 5.00 pm. By 1930, it was once again the Swinton cars, and not the Boothstown locals, which ran through to Leigh on Saturdays.

Between Swinton and Moses Gate, cars operated every

Plate 55. At the Bolton end of the through service from Leigh, cars terminated at Great Moor Street, where there was a covered shed and waiting shelter. Ex-Farnworth car No.53 waits to leave for Leigh Market whilst Bolton car No.30, allocated to the Westhoughton route, stands beneath the canopy.
G.N.Southerden.

11 minutes from the start of service at 4.44 a.m., until about 7.30 a.m.; then every eighteen minutes until 2.00 p.m. after which a 12-minute frequency operated until the end of service at 10.30 p.m. from Swinton and 11 .00 p.m. from Moses Gate. Journey time was half an hour. On Saturdays, the service started twenty minutes earlier and ended forty minutes later: the early morning service until 7.30 a.m. was less frequent than on Mondays to Fridays, and at irregular intervals. The service from *Black Horse* to Bolton, operated mostly by Bolton Corporation, ran every ten minutes throughout the day, from around 5.00 a.m. to 11.20 p.m., but was augmented to a five-minute frequency from 4.30 to 7.30 p.m. on Mondays to Fridays, and from noon on Saturdays.

The service between Walkden and *Black Horse* via Little Hulton and Longcauseway began at 5.00 a.m. from Walkden, but the next car was 5.30. and after a few more journeys at irregular intervals, cars ran every 24 minutes until 2.00 p.m. and then every 20 minutes until close of service. On Saturdays the service was increased: the first car left Walkden at 4.15 a.m., and cars ran approximately every 15 minutes until 6.00 a.m., when a fourteen-minute frequency began which lasted until noon, after which a

12-minute service was in force until the last car left Walkden at 10.48, half an hour later than Mondays to Fridays. A peculiarity of the timetable on this service was that some departures from *Black Horse* were given to the half-minute. This service was still linked operationally with *Black Horse* to Clifton (Newtown) and most cars ran through, changing the destination indicator at *Black Horse*. Obviously frequencies were the same, but each change of frequency naturally took place up to half an hour later than on the Little Hulton section.

On Sundays, services on nearly all routes began about 9.00 a.m., and operated half-hourly in the mornings, except that there was no service until mid-day on the Walkden-LittleHulton-*Black Horse*, *Black Horse*-Clifton, and *Black Horse*-Moses Gate sections. From about 1.00 p.m. a 15-minute service operated on the Atherton-Ashton and Atherton-Swinton routes; a 10 minute service on Lowton St. Mary's to Four Lane Ends, and a 12-minute service on Walkden-Little Hutton-*Black Horse*-Newtown, and Swinton-Walkden-Moses Gate.

In 1925 a large brick waiting room and enquiry office was built at Atherton, Punch Bowl, facing the end of Wigan Road.

Plate 56. S.L.T. No.53 picks up passengers as it leaves Great Moor Street en route to Leigh about 1930. Apparently, it was Bolton's request that the large bogie cars were used on this service, and it is thought that two additional cars (S.L.T. Nos.44 & 45), virtually identical with the re-built ex-Farnworth cars, appeared in 1927 as a result of this demand.
Dr. Hugh Nicol.

Plate 57. All but two of the ex-Farnworth cars received top-covers in the mid-1920s, and it is thought that seven were re-bodied. S.L.T No.56 has returned to its original tracks as it waits to reverse at the *Black Horse*, Farnworth, about 1926 on the joint service to Bolton. *Charles Wilkinson.*

Plate 58. Through running via Four Lane Ends into Bolton had been suspended 'temporarily' during the difficult days in 1915. It did not resume until 1927, when S.L.T. alone restored a Leigh to Bolton service. Ex-Farnworth bogie car No.58 is at Four Lane Ends, destination LEIGH MARKET. The driver, in summer uniform, leans on his controller as he surveys the cameraman. *M.J.O'Connor.*

The mystery of Bag Lane

As mentioned earlier, the short Bag Lane route was down to only five advertised journeys per week as early as 1908, but it has been impossible to find out when regular services ceased. It appears fairly certain that for some years after withdrawal of regular tram services, cars still operated to Bag Lane station at holiday times, and a car was run once every three months to make sure that the Company's operating rights did not lapse. It has sometimes been said that the line was finally abandoned in 1915, but this cannot be proved. What does seem certain is that the points connecting it to Market Street, and the right-angle crossing over Mealhouse Lane, were removed about 1915, leaving only the connecting curve into Mealhouse Lane. The Official Returns of the Ministry of Transport are no great help, as there are so many discrepancies and inexplicable variations in the mileage totals that it is almost impossible to reach any useful conclusions from them. However, it appears likely that Bag Lane was removed from the mileage figures in 1925. From the Ordnance Survey plans it seems that the track was still in position, not covered over, in 1927. Soon after that it was buried under tarmac - though normally companies are required to remove disused track - and it remained buried until revealed by road works in 1969.

New connections

In the late twenties, when the abandonment of the tramways was already a distinct probability, several useful connections were put in, and a number of through services introduced, which would have been far more useful twenty years earlier, before motor-bus services had developed.

New through services at Swinton and at Moses Gate

In the spring of 1926, a double-track connection was laid at Swinton between the S.L.T. tracks and the tracks owned by Swinton & Pendlebury U.D.C. and leased to Salford Corporation. The new connection - only about ten yards long - was first used on Monday 29th March, when an S.L.T. tram made a trial trip to Manchester (Deansgate), and a Salford tram to Walkden.

On Monday, 3rd May 1926, the Swinton-Walkden-Moses Gate tram service was replaced by two new services: Manchester (Deansgate) to Walkden, and Walkden to Bolton. They did not last long without interruption, for the General Strike began the following day, and no trams operated anywhere on the system until 14th May, after which things quickly returned to normal. This was the only strike ever to affect the S.L.T. until after the Second World War.

The new service between Manchester (Deansgate) and Walkden was operated jointly by Salford and the S.L.T.; Salford allocated the service number 61 to it. For a short distance in Deansgate and its approaches, the service travelled over tracks owned by Manchester Corporation. As neither Manchester nor Salford would allow cars bearing external advertisements to operate in their cities, the S.L.T. cars working this service had to be cleared of advertisements. Journey time was 50 minutes, and a fifteen-minute service ran throughout the day, starting at 5.00 a.m.from Manchester and 5.25 a.m. from Walkden: there were a few earlier local journeys between Swinton and Walkden. On Saturdays frequency was increased to ten minutes from mid-day; the last cars from Manchester were 10.15 p.m. Mondays to Fridays,10.50 p.m. Saturdays; the last from Walkden was 11 .10 p.m. daily. On Sundays the first through car left Deansgate at 9.10 a.m. and Walkden at 10.00 a.m. and a twenty-minute service ran until 2.00 p.m. followed by a ten-minute service. It is not possible to work out from the timetable the number of cars provided by each of the two operators, but it is believed that on Mondays to Fridays the S.L.T. provided three and Salford five. The through fare from Deansgate to Walkden was 6d.; there were, however, only a few through bookings and most passengers from intermediate stages had to re-book at Swinton church.

The through Walkden to Bolton service, with a journey time of half an hour, was at first operated solely by the S.L.T., but one Bolton car was put on the service from 6th December. Bolton used the same route letter "F" as for the Farnworth service. The fare was 4d., but although through bookings existed to the Bolton terminus (Great Moor Street), some passengers had to re-book at Moses Gate in theory, though in practice both tickets were issued at once. The original timetable started with the 5.10 a.m. from Walkden, and operated every 20 minutes until 6.50 a.m. when a ten-minute service began and continued throughout the day, the last car being 10.30 p.m. from Walkden and 11.00 p.m. from Bolton. On Saturdays the service continued twenty minutes later. On Sundays a service was provided between Walkden and Moses Gate by an L.U.T. motor-bus until the first tram left Walkden for Bolton at 11.50 a.m. A ten-minute service operated from 1.06 p.m. to 10.06 p.m. (10.36 from Bolton).

About the time these new through services were introduced, the frequency on the Walkden-Little Hulton-*Black Horse* and *Black Horse*-Newtown sections was increased from every 20 minutes to 15 minutes on Sunday to Friday afternoons, and a Sunday morning bus service was introduced between Moses Gate, *Black Horse,* Newtown, and Pendlebury.

Farnworth lease renewed

The lease of the Farnworth tramways was due to expire on 31st March 1927. By an agreement signed on 2nd February 1926, the lease was renewed for a further 21 years, though not until after considerable discussion in Farnworth Council, many of whose members would have preferred to lease the undertaking to Bolton instead. Under the new agreement, the Company was to continue operation and maintenance; the Council was to receive 5% of the net receipts. The Company was to continue to purchase from the Council all the current needed for tramway operation in Farnworth, Clifton, Kearsley, and Little Hulton. The whole of the track was to be relaid by 1932: this task was started right away. Moses Gate to *Black Horse* was relaid between May and October 1926, using asphalt instead of granite setts for the paving. In the process, the complex layout at Moses Gate was much simplified, and all the connecting curves allowing through running from *Black Horse* towards Walkden, and vice versa, were removed. Longcauseway was relaid in 1927. The old tram depot in Albert Road reverted to the Council, who continued to lease it to the existing sub-lessees. A new agreement between the S.L.T. and Kearsley U.D.C. was signed on 10th August 1926. For the first time, eventual abandonment was publicly envisaged. The lease of the few yards belonging to Kearsley in Longcauseway and Higher Market Street, including the junction, was renewed for 21 years from 1st April 1927, but the "main line" from the corner of Longcauseway to the boundary at Unity Brook was leased for four years only. If the company decided by 31st March 1931 not to let the lease expire, they were to renew it for a further 17 years, and relay the track, either doubling it or retaining single-track, but in any case replacing the centre poles by side poles and span wires. Following the new agreement, there was a re-arrangement of the working of the Farnworth tramways. The S.L.T. withdrew entirely from the Bolton-*Black Horse* service, probably from 1st April 1927. From this date also, the S.L.T. share in the Bolton-Walkden service was reduced to one car: within a year or two this had been further reduced to one car on Saturdays only.

Plate 59. Of the thirteen ex-Farnworth cars, eleven were fitted with canopy top-covers in the period 1923-26, and some were re-bodied. Only No.51 & 52 remained in open-top state. Car No.44, allegedly built new to the same design, is seen on the Bolton service in August 1933.

M.J.O'Connor, courtesy A.D.Packer.

Plate 60. Bogie car No.54 pauses to collect passengers on Leigh Road, outside Atherton Depot. The newer brickwork of the 1926 depot extension may be noted.

Dr. Hugh Nicol.

Trolleybuses authorised: S.L.T. ACT 1929

By this time, it was obvious that extensive track and rolling stock renewals would be needed soon. On parts of the system there was hardly enough traffic to justify such expenditure now that there were efficient alternatives to the tramcar for lightly-loaded routes. On the busiest route, track doubling was desirable in order to improve both the speed and regularity of the service, yet many sections of road were too narrow for double track. Track maintenance in the many areas affected by mining subsidence was difficult. On the other hand the Company did not want to write off the considerable capital involved in the power station and the distribution system. In these circumstances the obvious solution was to introduce trolleybuses, which had recently greatly improved from their former primitive tram-like state. The superior acceleration and quiet operation of trolleybuses were much more noticeable in comparison with contemporary motor-buses than is the case nowadays. In fact Mr. Edwardes had been considering trolleybus conversion as early as 1922, but at that time trolleybuses were still very slow and rough-riding.

By an Act of 10th May 1929 (19 & 20 Geo.V, cap lxxxiii) the name of the company was changed to South Lancashire Transport, and it was authorised to abandon its tramway routes, and to operate trolley-buses over all its own tramway routes (except Leigh to Lowton Old Terminus) and also over the routes of the Farnworth Council Tramways, Kearsley Council Tramways, and Barton R.D.C. Light Railways. These three authorities could, if they wished, erect the necessary equipment themselves, and lease it to the Company. The following trolleybus extensions were also authorised: Lowton St. Mary's to Lowton Lane Head, and Clifton boundary (Newtown) to the top of Station Road, Pendlebury. The Company was also authorised to operate motor-buses within fifteen miles of Leigh Town Hall, with a few minor exceptions. Various clauses giving local authorities the power to purchase the parts of the undertaking in their territories were repealed, but an attempt by the Company to shed its street-lighting responsibilities failed in the face of opposition from the local authorities.

In changing its name from "Tramways" to "Transport", the S.L.T. was following the example of its parent company, for the L.U.T. had changed its name to "Lancashire United Transport & Power Co., Ltd." in 1928 in recognition of its expanding motor-bus interests. Incidentally, the L.U.T. was at this period a dealer in motor-cars and various types of electrical equipment: it also installed private telephone systems.

Of the two trolleybus extensions authorised by the Act, the one at Lowton is difficult to understand, for as Leigh to Lowton Old Terminus was specifically excepted from the trolleybus powers, the section Old Terminus to St. Mary's, and the new extension to Lane Head would have been quite isolated had they ever been equipped for trolleybuses. Presumably it was hoped that Leigh Corporation would obtain trolleybus powers for the "missing link". The other new extension, at Newtown, would provide a more convenient terminus than the former tram terminus at the boundary. It will be remembered that for twenty years there had been a gap of some 200 yards between the S.L.T. (Barton-on-Irwell R.D.C.) and Salford Corporation (Swinton & Pendlebury U.D.C.) tracks at this point. This gap was closed at the eleventh hour of the tramways, when a new double- track connection, belonging to Swinton & Pendlebury U.D.C., was constructed in July 1928. To make better connection with the S.L.T., some Salford Corporation cars were diverted from Station Road on to this connection for a time (some records say from 30th January to 10th March 1929, but other accounts are contradictory). It seems that after this, S. L. T. services were extended over the new connection instead, to the *Windmill*.

Plate 62. The planned conversion of the Atherton-Farnworth route to trolleybus operation, spelt the end for the joint Walkden-Manchester service, on which trams ran for the last time on 18th February 1931. Pending the completion of the conversion work, the Swinton-Walkden section was covered by a shuttle service until 18th August 1931, with trolleybuses taking over the following day. Car No.59, seen in final form at Swinton, was allocated to the shuttle service on 23rd July 1931.

G.N.Southerden.

The last new tram service

On Saturday 1st February 1930, a through joint service was introduced between Manchester (Deansgate) and Farnworth (*Black Horse*). Salford Corporation allocated route number 74 but it is doubtful if it was ever actually displayed on the cars. The service ran to Moses Gate for the first week or so, on Mondays to Fridays, but was soon curtailed to the *Black Horse*. It is difficult to understand why the service was ever introduced at all, as a bus service to Manchester was already running every twelve minutes along the same route.

The journey time from *Black Horse* to Manchester varied between 45 and 50 minutes: all through passengers had to re-book at Pendlebury except those travelling only a very short distance, for whom there was a special cross-boundary 1d. fare.

It is believed there were several alterations in the detailed timetable during the brief life of this service, but in January 1931 the service was as follows: a shuttle service ran every 25 minutes in the morning between Pendlebury and *Black Horse*, starting at 4.56 from Pendlebury (S.L.T. cars entering service at Pendlebury would have to reverse twice, at Swinton Church to get from Partington Lane into Station Road, and again at Pendlebury to run towards Farnworth). Through service started at 7.56 a.m. from *Black Horse* and 8.11 a.m. from Deansgate, and ran every half-hour until mid-day, when a 15-minute service began; the last through cars were 10.23 from *Black Horse* and 10.26 p.m. from Deansgate. On Saturdays, the early morning shuttle service started at 4.56 from *Black Horse* instead of Pendlebury, the cars entering service via Walkden, but otherwise the only change from the Monday to Friday service was that there was one later car from Deansgate. On Sundays there was no through service at Pendlebury: during the morning a 20-minute service was provided by buses between *Black Horse* and Pendlebury, and a 15-minute tram service, requiring four cars, began at *Black Horse* at 12.23 p.m. and ended at Pendlebury at 11.02 p.m.

From the timetable, it would appear that the through service required two S.L.T. and five Salford cars to maintain the 15-minute frequency, but the Saturday service appears to require four S.L.T. and three Salford cars. However, this is unlikely, as there would not be enough S.L.T. cars without advertisements.

Plate 63, left. After the conversion of the Atherton-Farnworth route, only the Leigh-Bolton tram services remained. Car No.4, seen at Great Moor Street, Bolton, in February 1933 was one of the single-truck cars which remained in service until the end of tramway operation. The last S.L.T. trams ran on Saturday 16th December 1933.

M.J.O'Connor, courtesy A.D.Packer.

Plate 64, right. Ex-Farnworth car No.57 stands at the Great Moor Street terminus, Bolton, operating a short-working of the Leigh route as far as Hulton Lane, some way short of Four Lane Ends. After the resumption of through running on the Leigh-Bolton service in 1927, Bolton cars worked only as far as Daubhill station with occasional extras to Hulton Lane. *M.J.O'Connor, courtesy A.D.Packer.*

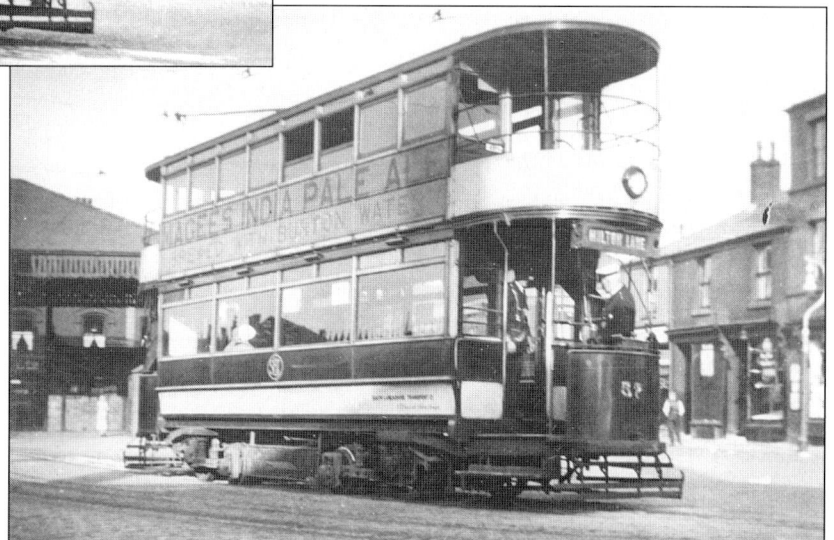

Conversion to the trolleybus

Conversion of the Atherton-Ashton service to trolleybus operation was complete by 3rd August 1930, and the Ashton-Haydock section (delayed by the construction of a bridge to carry the new East Lancashire Road, A580) began on 21st June 1931, simultaneously with the conversion of St. Helens Corporation's Haydock route. (St. Helens had begun to abandon its tramways for trolleybuses in 1927, whilst Wigan opted in favour of motor buses.) On 28th February 1931 Wigan trams ran to Hindley for the last time. This was the last day of operation of the through tram services between Farnworth *(Black Horse)* and Manchester and between Walkden and Manchester, though a reduced tram service continued to operate from Farnworth as far as Pendlebury until 7th June 1931. For a while the Swinton-Walkden section was operated as a separate shuttle service, but the last trams on this section and on the Atherton-Swinton and Walkden-Little Hulton-*Black Horse* routes ran on the 18th August 1931.

The Atherton-Farnworth service was one of the longest trolleybus routes ever operated in this country, being exceeded only by the 14½-mile route of the Nottinghamshire & Derbyshire Traction Company between Nottingham and Ripley (operated 1933 to 1953). and route 630 of London Transport from Croydon to "Near Willesden Junction", 14¾ miles, (1937 to 1960). The journey time from Atherton to Farnworth varied from 68 to 71 minutes, and a 20-minute frequency operated in the mornings, increasing to 15 minutes in the afternoons. For the first couple of years a 12-minute service operated on Saturday afternoon and evening.

Most of the trolleybuses for this service were based on Swinton depot, but three operated from Atherton depot. These had to travel between the depot and the *Punch Bowl,* when entering or leaving service, with one trolley on the tram wire and a "skate" trailing on the tramtrack: it seems that contrary to the usual practice elsewhere, where the wiring of the vehicles provided for switching to "earth return", the S.L.T. used a special short bamboo pole, with insulated cable attached, to provide connection between the "idle" trolley, hooked down to the roof, and the skate attached to the rear of the vehicle. Later, when trolleybus overhead was erected between the Depot and the *Punch Bowl* slightly in advance of the rest of the Leigh-Bolton section, operation of the Farnworth service was shared more evenly between Atherton and Swinton depots.

The opening of this trolleybus service also inevitably led to the withdrawal of the one remaining S.L.T. Saturdays-only car from the Bolton-Walkden service, leaving operation entirely to Bolton Corporation. In return, in order to "balance the mileage" of operation on each other's tracks, S.L.T. cars now occasionally appeared on the local services between Bolton, Hulton Lane, and Four Lane Ends, entirely on Bolton Corporation tracks.

A curious incident occurred in Farnworth on Sunday 20th December 1931. Following the sudden failure of a span wire, half a mile of tramway overhead collapsed into the street, causing great alarm among passers-by ! Several Bolton Corporation cars were stranded on the Farnworth side of the break, and services were not restored until late the following day.

Plate 65. Trams had vanished from the Atherton-Farnworth service to be replaced on this long and circuitous journey by trolleybuses. S.L.T. No.11, supplied by Guy in 1931, was still in fundamentally original condition when photographed at Worsley Court House in 1947. *E.Gray.*

Plate 66. The last tramcar to enter the depot on 16th December 1933 was No.7, which had been driven from Leigh by General Manager Mr. E.H.Edwardes (centre with cap and moustache). At a celebrarory dinner a few days later, the Bolton Manager announced that he wished success to the new trolleybuses, but that he had no intention of scrapping his trams.

End of tramway operation

Apart from the sections operated by other tramway undertakings (Moses Gate to Walkden and *Black Horse,* and Worsley to Winton), the Atherton-Farnworth conversion left only the Lowton-Leigh and Leigh-Bolton tram services in operation. The last S.L.T. trams ran on Saturday 16th December 1933. The following day, S.L.T. trolleybuses began to work between Leigh and Bolton, whilst the Lowton route was covered by a joint Lancashire United and Leigh Corporation motor bus service.

The last tram from Four Lane Ends to the Depot, leaving at 11.45 p.m. on 16th December, was driven by Mr. T. Wilson; one of the oldest employees. The last car to reach the Depot was No.7, leaving Leigh at 11.55 p.m. driven by Mr. Edwardes. Incidentally, Mr. Edwardes was now Managing Director, not just General Manager, having been appointed to the Company's Board in 1932. Fares collected on these two journeys were given to Leigh Infirmary, and the last ticket on each car was auctioned, the proceeds being donated to the same cause. Notices announcing the arrangements were headed "The Last Jolt", but few passengers can have understood the Latin

sub-heading "Gaudeamus Igitur" ("Therefore we rejoice") as no translation was provided! The notice concluded with the verse:

> Come and have a Ride - on the Last One
> Try and keep your Seat - if you get one
> Kindly take your mind back - speak nicely little man,
> Of the pioneers of Transport - and the South Lancs. tram.

The writers of doggerel verse had also been busy on the last cars, one of which bore the inscription:

> "Farewell, my old and trusted friend,
> No more this way you'll roam,
> For after to-night we'll have to fight,
> For a bus when we want to go home."
> "How canst thou bear to leave me?
> Dost know thy parting grieves me?
> Thou goest. Whate'er befall me,
> On foggy nights I'll call thee.
> Farewell, farewell, my own true friend,

Plate 71. Of the cars purchased by Bolton from S.L.T. in 1933, most saw service for another thirteen years. In 1940, all Bolton trams had 300 added to their fleet numbers. Well-loaded car No.338, complete with wartime headlamp masks and white fenders for the blackout, works the Farnworth route. *Courtesy A.D.Packer.*

Plate 72. In this 1945 view of Bolton car No.340, the photographer appears to have perpetrated a little joke by turning the destination screen to read ALBERT ROAD, location of the original 1901 Farnworth depot. *C.E.Box.*

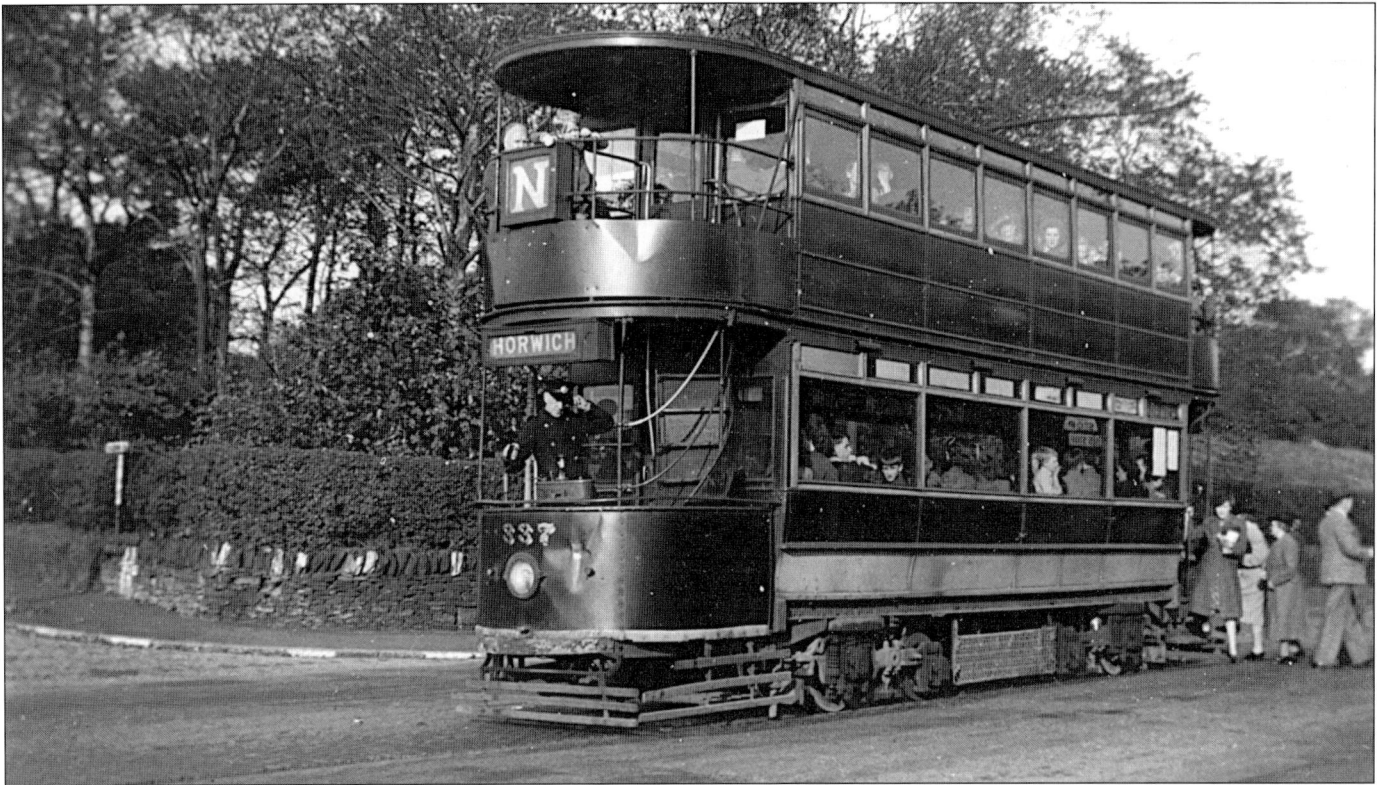

Plate 73. After the closure of the Farnworth route in 1944, the ex-S.L.T. bogie cars were used on the long route to Horwich, on which, despite their old-fashioned bodies, their powerful equipment proved an advantage. Car No.337 was photographed in October 1946. Bolton trams ceased to operate in March 1947, by which date all the former S.L.T. cars had been scrapped.

M.J.O'Connor, courtesy A.D.Packer.

Plate 74. In post-war years, the S.L.T. trolleybus fleet was in urgent need of renewal, as was much of the overhead equipment. Minor improvements were carried out, including the fitting of more modern front ends to some vehicles, but the dated appearance generally, gave away their 1930s origins. In August 1955 it was announced that the trolleybuses were to be replaced by motor buses. A reprieve due to the Suez crisis (and the threat to oil supplies) in 1956 allowed operation to continue for a further two years. The Atherton-Farnworth service was the last survivor, closing on 31st August 1958. No.45, little altered from its original condition, is seen at Worsley. When new, the four-wheel trolleys were intended for the Leigh-Bolton service, but because of their low seating capacity, were transferred to other routes.

E.Gray.

CHAPTER 6. TRAMWAY ROLLING STOCK

Altogether the S.L.T. owned 93 tramcars during its 31 years of tramway operation. This includes the cars taken over from Farnworth Council Tramways and from Lancashire Light Railways. Most of the fleet were single-truck (i.e. four-wheel) cars but fifteen were bogie vehicles. Most of the Company's records were destroyed for salvage during the Second World War, so the details, particularly of rebuilds and similar alterations, have had to be pieced together from photographs and the few surviving records, and there remains much to be discovered. Unfortunately, some sources are contradictory: for instance a document purporting to list the capital expenditure on rolling stock, prepared in connection with the submission to Parliament of the S.L.T. Bill 1929, cannot be fully reconciled in its details with the English Electric Company's records of what they supplied. Further, information provided by Mr. Edwardes shortly before his retirement, and presumably based on memory, does not agree with either.

Considering that the St. Helens company was one of the first to provide windscreens to protect the driver from the elements, it seems odd that the S.L.T. never provided any such protection throughout its whole period of tramway operation. It was, of course, not alone in this, but one would have thought that with much the same administration, both companies would have provided this 'luxury'. Nor were any of the S.L.T.'s cars ever provided with a fully-enclosed top-deck. Many cars were provided with top covers, but the end balconies were always left open to the weather. It is extraordinary that this feature was retained on cars built as late as 1927. Another feature always lacking on the S.L.T., but very common on most systems of any size, was the magnetic brake, that very efficient tramcar brake which can bring the car to an almost immediate dead stand by virtually clamping it to the rails through a brake shoe applied to the track in the form of an electro-magnet: however the S.L.T. was in good company in neglecting this device, for Manchester did not use it either.

Milnes single-truck cars, Nos. 1-45

These forty-five open-top four-wheel cars were supplied in 1902 by G. F. Milnes & Co., Ltd., of Hadley, Shropshire, for the opening of the first sections. This firm, whose origins go back to George Starbuck's 'tramway carriage manufactory' founded in 1862, had moved from Birkenhead to Hadley, Shropshire, in 1899, after the company had been re-organised and come under German control in 1898. The Atherton brothers were important shareholders, so it is not surprising that this firm received the order.

The cars were mounted on 6-ft. wheelbase girder trucks of the type standardised by Milnes, but actually manufactured at Bautzen in Saxony by their German associate, the Busch Waggon-und Maschinenfabrik AG. The electrical equipment, supplied by Messrs Witting, Eborall, of London, was manufactured by the Socie'te' Anonyme Electricite et Hydraulique of Charleroi, Belgium (now Ateliers de Constructions Electriques de Charleroi).

The bodies were genuine Milnes productions. The lower deck, l6ft between bulkheads, had three side windows, each with two small hinged ventilation windows above. In accordance with the usual practice of the period, most of these small hinged lights were coloured and engraved with an ornamental pattern, but some bore advertisements instead. Subsequently, they were mostly replaced by plain glass. There were seats for 22 passengers on longitudinal seats. The platforms were of course 'unvestibuled', i.e. without windscreens or similar protection. Milnes 'exhibition' stairs, which turned through about 95º, were fitted. The platform entrance could be closed by a 'lazy-tongs' gate, and on the off-side of the platform, beneath the stairs, was a gate or ornamental scroll-work. On the open upper deck were seats for 33 passengers; these comprised seven rows of 'two and two' reversible 'garden' seats, except for a single seat alongside the trolley-standard which was mounted slightly off-centre, and an inwards-facing fixed seat for three persons on each canopy. The headlamp was mounted on the canopy end. The original destination indicators consisted of a rotating hexagonal board, lettered in black on white, mounted on the canopy endrails. About 1906, these were replaced by roller-blind indicators of the more usual form, lettered in white on black, and of course capable of displaying a greater number of destinations.

The cars were fitted with two 25 h.p. motors, but these were soon found to be inadequate, and were later replaced by more powerful motors, reputedly 45 h.p.

About 1903, car no.3 was fitted experimentally with a 'Magrini' top cover, supplied by Messrs. G.C. Milnes, Voss and Company, of Birkenhead; G. C. Milnes was the son of G.F. Milnes, but the two companies were not in any way associated. This type of cover had originally been developed, like Liverpool's 'Bellamy' top-cover which it closely resembled, as a light-weight collapsible affair, by which cars could quickly be converted from open-top to covered-top as weather conditions required. In practice there turned out to be little demand for the convertible arrangement, and most Magrini covers, though retaining the advantages of light weight and easy fitting and removal were permanent fixtures. Like most

Plate 75. Milnes single-truck car No.2 of the 1 to 45 series delivered in 1902, is seen at Mosley Common. The car is in original condition, apart from the roller blind destination screen, which has replaced the rotating box fitted on delivery.

of these covers, the one fitted to No.3 had a domed roof and did not extend over the canopies. Almost certainly the original trolley-standard was retained, projecting through the roof of the new top-cover. The fitting of this cover was probably the result of a Milnes Voss offer to fit a cover to one car for £50 and remove it again at their own expense: however, in this case it did not lead to further orders and seems to have been removed quite soon. There are rumours that the cover was too high for certain bridges and had to be altered, but it seems unlikely that the Company would have specified the wrong height. There is no evidencethat any other S. L.T. cars were fitted with top-covers at this period.

In 1914, a start was made on fitting top covers to the class. Twenty top-covers were purchased in 1914 and five in 1915. It is understood, but cannot now be confirmed, that these came from the Brush Electrical Engineering Co., Ltd., of Loughborough. They had six drop windows each side, almost square, and each one with a small fixed window above. The roof extended over the canopies, but these were left open-ended in the form of balconies. The seating was increased from 55 to 58 in the process: in the absence of a trolley-standard now that the trolley could be mounted on the roof, the single seat was replaced by a double, and the end seats for three were replaced by seats for four, curving round the balcony, and still, of course, facing inwards. The destination indicators were removed from the canopy rail to below the canopy. As already mentioned, the fitting of top covers was carried out at Platt Bridge depot.

There is now no record of which twenty-five cars received top-covers, but from photographic evidence it is known that this first batch included No.8 and probably No. 19.

Soon after the first cars had been fitted with top covers it was found that the short wheelbase girder trucks were insufficient to take the increased weight of the bodies. In 1919 the English Electric Co., Ltd., of Preston, supplied 74 truck side frames of 7ft-6in wheelbase, of the Brill '21-E' type, and 37 cars were accordingly re-trucked. Of the eight cars retaining the original trucks, it can be fairly safely supposed that six were numbers 15, 16, 23, 27, 41, and 43, but the other two cannot be identified: they may have been 22 and 45, or possibly 37 and 40.

New bogie cars Nos. 44-45

Two new bogie cars identical with the re-bodied and top-covered version of the ex-Farnworth cars were supplied by English Electric in 1927, and numbered 44 and 45, taking the numbers of withdrawn single-truck cars They had Burnley bogies built by the Electro-Mechanical Brake Co., Ltd, General Electric motors, and English Electric K33C controllers. The English Electric records give the seating as 44 on the upper deck and 34 on the lower, but in fact they seem to have had the same 52 seats on the upper deck as the former Farnworth cars.

It is a pity that the opportunity was not taken to build cars of a more up-to-date type with fully enclosed top covers and vestibuled platforms. The only concession to modernity was upholstered seats in the lower saloon. The two cars cost £1,892 each. Only number 45 (not 44) had upholstery. This is believed to be the first-ever use of foam rubber in a public transport vehicle.*

(Editor's note: It is fair to add that at least one distinguished transport historian has queried the origin of the two 'new' vehicles numbered 44 and 45. He found it inconceivable that in 1927 any self-respecting tramcar manufacturer would construct vehicles to a 25 year -old outmoded design.)

Disposals

All fifteen bogie cars were still in service until 1930, but although the Official Returns show two cars as withdrawn in that year, there is conflicting evidence as to which two cars these were. One would expect them to be the remaining open-top cars, 51-52, but this is by no means certain. The remaining thirteen were in service to the end. After acquisition by the S. L. T. in 1906, some of the bogie cars had been used on the Atherton-Haydock service, but it is not certain what routes they usually worked subsequently; in the final years they normally worked the through services to Bolton and Manchester, and Nos. 46, 53, and 57, as well as the new cars 44 and 45, were cleared of external advertisements for the latter service. Number 53 was withdrawn in 1932, but the others remained in service until the end of tramway operation in 1933.

With the cessation of tramway operation by the S. L. T. at the end of 1933, eight bogie cars (numbers 44,45,47,48,50,54,55 and 58) were sold to Bolton

Plate 79, previous page. Extensively re-built by S.L.T. during the 1920s, eight of the ex-Farnworth bogie cars were purchased by Bolton in 1933, the working life of some extended by over twelve years. A side-view of one of the cars in its final form may be compared with the 1901 version in the previous illustration. When the top-covers were fitted, the reverse stairs were replaced by the more usual 180 degree pattern. Bolton No.40 stands under the trolleybus wires by the Hulton Lane crossover in June 1935.   *A.M.Gunn.*

Corporation. They became Bolton numbers 33 to 40, but it is not known in what order, though the new cars of 1927 are thought to have become 33 and 40. It can be assumed safely that the remaining six were cars which had been rebodied in the twenties: indeed, photographic evidence confirms this. They were thoroughly overhauled before entering service. Magnetic track brakes were added to the trucks. The headlamp was moved to the dash, and a large indicator box for the route letter was added to the balcony rails. The destination indicator had already been moved from the canopy rails to a position beneath the canopy by the S.L.T. during overhauls and rebuilding. A destination indicator was also installed on the side: at first this was suspended in one of the windows, but subsequently the box was fitted in the half-light nearest the platform.

Nos 33 and 38 were scrapped in 1939. In 1940, like all other trams in Bolton, the remainder had 300 added to their numbers. In 1945, the motors from the scrapped No.38 were fitted to Bolton No.451 (ex Bury No.55).

When first transferred to Bolton, these cars worked principally on the service to Hulton Lane and Four Lane Ends, but soon migrated to the *Black Horse* line. After abandonment of the Farnworth route in 1944, they worked mostly on the long Horwich route, where their powerful equipment was an advantage despite their old-fashioned bodies: the route had previously been worked by totally-enclosed cars. From about 1944, as on all Bolton cars, carbon skids replaced the trolley wheels, after a trolleybus skid borrowed from the S. L. T. had been tried experimentally.

After abandonment of the Horwich route on 6th October 1946, these cars saw little use, but some were still in existence in December, e.g. No.334. No.336 was scrapped in May 1946. By the time the last Bolton trams ran in March 1947, all these cars had been scrapped.

Single-truck cars Nos. 59-82 Brush/U.E.C.

Twenty-four single-truck top-covered cars, costing £545 each, were delivered in 1906. However, there are conflicting reports about their manufacturer. According to Mr. Edwardes, they were supplied by the United Electric Car Co., Ltd., of Preston. This firm had been formed in 1905, when the Electric Railway and Tramway Carriage Works Ltd., (formerly Dick, Kerr) purchased the goodwill of the British Electric Car Co., Ltd., of Trafford Park, and of G. F. Milnes & Co., Ltd. The U.E.C. became English Electric in 1918. Some contemporary newspaper reports, on the other hand, state that some of the class were built by Brush at Loughborough and some by the U.E.C. The most detailed information is to be found in the *Light Railway and Tramway Journal* which stated that the order had been placed with British Thomson-Houston and sub-contracted by them: they ordered 24 trucks and

14 bodies from Brush. Presumably the other bodies were built by the U.E.C. All photographs so far seen of these cars in original condition show bodywork features usually thought to be of definite Brush origin, for instance six 'scoop' ventilators on each side just above the lower-deck windows: three ventilators facing in each direction. However, as far as can be ascertained the cars from No.73 onwards differed in certain details from the remainder, so the *Light Railway and Tramway Journal* may well have been correct

The trucks were of the Brush 'A' 7ft-6in type, built by the Brush Company as sub-contractor for British Thompson-Houston. The lower decks were virtually identical with the Milnes cars of the 1-45 class, but naturally with detail differences. The small panes above the window were fixed from the beginning. They had 180° stairs.

All the cars were top-covered from the beginning, but the original covers were lightweight affairs, similar in appearance to the then well-known 'Bellamy' type, with no roof over the canopies. They were, however, permanent fixtures and not removable as were 'Bellamy' topcovers. There were three large windows each side, with no small panes above. The destination indicator boxes were hung below the canopies. Seating is believed to have been 58: 22 on the lower deck and 36 on the upper. Later, some of the cars were rebuilt in the twenties with English Electric top-covers identical to those fitted to the Milnes cars: Nos 59, and 73 were definitely so fitted, and there must havebeen at least another five similarly altered. Some cars, (including nos 59, 62, and 73 already mentioned) appear to have received completely new bodies identical with those fitted to the 1-45 class, as photographs exist showing these cars with three "extractor" ventilators above the lower deck windows, instead of the six Brush-type 'air scoops' originally fitted, and exhibiting other detail differences from their original condition. The English Electric records make no reference to these.

All these cars were still in service in 1930: it is probable that all were withdrawn in 1930 and 1931, though one or two may have lingered until 1933.

Single-truck cars, ex L.L.R. Nos.83-89

These seven open-top single-truck cars comprised the total rolling stock of the Liverpool and Prescot line, and though owned by Lancashire Light Railways were numbered 37 to 43 in the New St. Helens Company's fleet. They were transferred to the S.L.T. when the Liverpool and Prescot was sold to Liverpool in 1919. Though sometimes claimed to be Milnes cars identical with the S.L.T.'s 1-45 class, the probability is that they were in fact built by the British Electric Car Co.,Ltd., and

differed considerably from the Milnes cars. The problem of identification of these cars is discussed further in Appendix II: so far no photographs have been discovered of S.L.T. cars 83 to 89: if any photograph does turn up, it will almost certainly solve the problem.

These cars seem to have been little used on the S. L. T. By 1924, Nos.84 and 86 had been scrapped, Nos.83 and 88 had been withdrawn but were still in existence (and still were in 1928),and No.89 had become a snowplough. The remaining two, Nos.85 and 87, were withdrawn about 1930. None received covered tops.

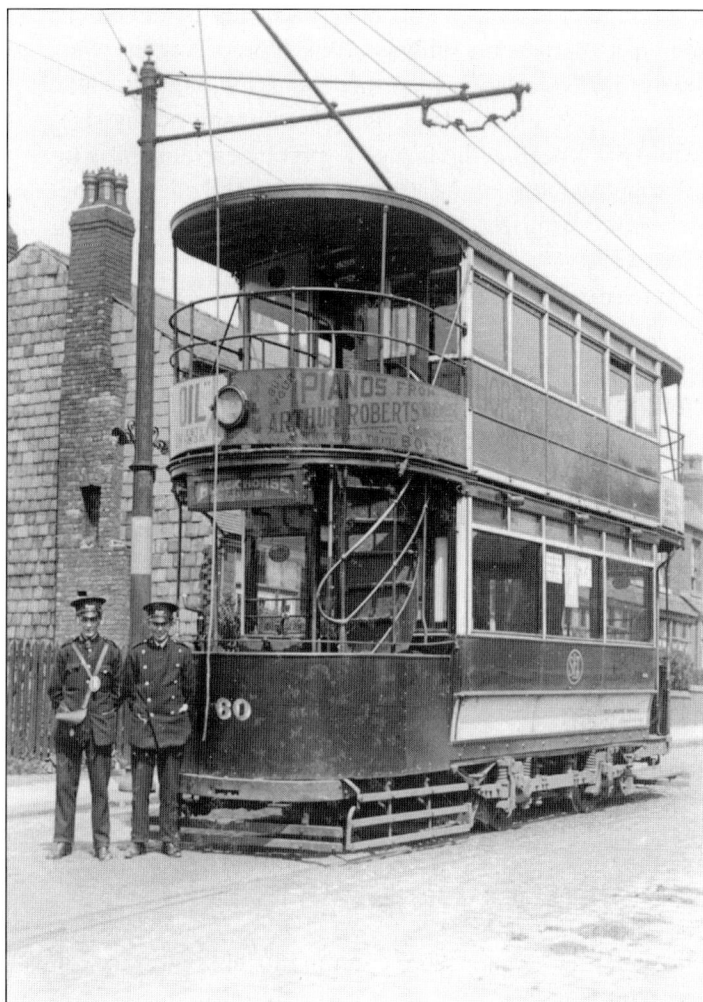

Plate 80. In the 1920s some of the 59-82 series cars were re-built, their original lightweight covers being replaced with balcony-type tops identical to those fitted on the earlier Milnes cars. Car No.60 again, in its final form, works the Farnworth (Black Horse) route in 1929. The distinctive Brush loop of the staircase handrail is clearly visible.
Dr. Hugh Nicol.

Single-deck car

This car is something of a mystery. Documents prepared in connection with the S.L.T. Bill of 1929 show that it was purchased in 1901 for the remarkably low price of £375, and was a single-truck car. It figured in the Official Returns until 1905/6, but it may be presumed to have continued in existence for a few more years, for an advertisement in the 1908 timetable booklet refers to a 'special saloon car', painted white, which could be hired for weddings, funerals, outings, etc; this 'special saloon car' can hardly have been any of the normal double-deck fleet.

Its original role seems to have been that of directors' saloon. Common on railways, this type of vehicle was always rare on tramways in this country, though no self-respecting American street railway company of any size would have been without such a 'private car', and it is to be supposed that the car was in fact the idea of the Atherton brothers with their claimed American experience.

There remains the problem of where it was kept if it was in fact purchased in 1901, as work on the S.L.T. depot did not begin until 1902. Secondly, £375 is far too low a price, even by the standards of the time, for a car which one would expect to be more luxuriously appointed than normal. Thirdly, why should such a car have been scrapped at an early date? One would expect it to have been rebuilt if it could not continue to fulfil its original role. And why did it apparently not take part in the ceremonial procession from Liverpool to Bolton in 1903? It was so different from the rest, that one would expect the newspaper reports to have mentioned it, especially as the reporters were observant enough to note the reversed stairs of the Liverpool Corporation cars in the procession. There is nothing to indicate that it could be the car 'painted yellow' in the procession, for apparently it was only its yellowness and not its shape which distinguished this car.

However, there is a possible solution, but it must be emphasised that it is only a theory, and no confirmation has yet come to light. In 1897, a demonstration track a quarter of a mile long was constructed at Prescot Cable Works (British Insulated Wire Co.) as briefly mentioned in chapter one, to demonstrate a new type of conduit current collection* developed by the Simplex Electric Tramway Conduit Syndicate Ltd., with which the Atherton brothers and the B.l.W. Co. were associated. To work this line, a single-truck single-deck car was

Plate 81. Car No.62 in its final form leaves Ashton-in-Makerfield for Atherton about 1928. The bracing rods supporting the top-deck, as used with the original top-covers, appear to have been retained on the re-roofed cars. *Dr. H.A.Whitcombe*

Appendix I. Tickets

This appendix was compiled principally from information supplied by Mr. W. H. Bett, supplemented by further details supplied by Mr. Cyril Kidd. The author is very grateful to these two gentlemen for their co-operation, and is further indebted to Mr. Kidd for allowing items from his collection to be illustrated: the numbers in brackets refer to the illustrations.

Like many transport undertakings, the S.L.T. started with 'full geographical' tickets, that is, tickets in which the stages are given in the form "Lowton to Leigh Market", the punch hole thus indicating the precise maximum journey possible by the passenger. The tickets were coded by colour, for instance 1d. white, 2d. green, 3d. blue, 4d. pale lemon, 5d. salmon. The earliest issues seem to have been printed by the Bell Punch Company (1), from whom ticket punches of the once familiar pattern were hired, though at an early date these were replaced by non-ringing, non-registering punches. Later tickets in the same style were printed by Williamson of Ashton-under-Lyne, and others by the Punch & Ticket Company.

Soon after the change of printer came a change from the original 'full geographical' style. Tickets now listed the stage points by name "out" on the left and "in" on the right, without indicating the precise journey. In common with earlier issues the route was indicated by an abbreviation in heavy type, in the centre column, for instance LB for "Lowton-Bolton", AS for "Atherton-Swinton", SN "Swinton-Newtown" - the AS replaced in 1909 by AMG "Atherton-Moses Gate".

Among special tickets were the workmen's tickets, at first both single and return, but in later years, return only. The earliest ones were 'fully geographical' (5). The return tickets were generally long white tickets with spaces for date and cancellation as well as stages. The week of the year was usually overprinted in green, red, or blue (varying according to the year). A specimen of a workman's single ticket is a salmon- coloured 1d. with a "WS" overprint. (6)

There was also a workmen's weekly ticket, a large pink form, apparently issued at the offices and not by conductors, as the fare was blank and had to be entered in manuscript. School children were able to obtain reduced rate tickets in booklets of 50, allowing them to travel for 1/2d. on a 1d.stage, for 1d. on a 2d. stage: for example a 1/2d. ticket is known, reading "To or from Atherton & Leigh Workhouse". Child return tickets also existed in 1d. and 11/2d. values, similar in design to workmen's tickets. Although the S.L.T. normally just cancelled return tickets by an appropriate punch-hole on the return journey, a 'Railway & Scholar's Exchange' ticket was used (9) as a no-fare-value ticket in exchange for the special children's tickets and in connection with the through bookings to Leigh from certain stations of the Great Central Railway (mentioned in chapter two).

Apart from the Four Lane Ends to Moses Gate via Worsley 'tourist' 9d. ticket, also valid as a Four Lane Ends-Worsley return,-and mentioned in chapter four, the only return tickets available to ordinary passengers were 3d. day returns for certain 2d. stages; all were red with a white stripe.

About the time of the first world war came tickets with numerical stages instead of names (2). These were in various colours, with outline fare overprints in black. The number of stages varied, and the rare changes of fares resulted in changes of colours and range of stages to suit, hence some apparent inconsistencies - among known varieties are 11/2d. white with stages 1,2,3 in and 4, 5,6 out, while another had stages 1 to 10a and 2a to 12; a 2d. blue with stages 1 to 8 in, 5 to 12 out; 21/2d. blue, stages 1 to 9 and 4 to 12; a 4d. buff, 1 to 5 and 8 to 12; a 4d. grey-brown with stages 1 to 7 and 6 to 12; 5d. pink, stages 1 to 5 and 8 to 12; 6d. salmon with the same stages as the 5d; 7d. lilac, with No.1 stage in and No.12 stage out.

Some of these tickets lingered until about 1930, but a different style had already been introduced in the mid-twenties. These tickets were white for all values with the fare indicated by means of large red overprint (3). All had stages 1 to 12 on the left and 13 to 24 on the right; this simplification of design not only reduced printing costs but avoided rendering existing stocks obsolete in case of fare alterations. The earliest printings had the "South Lancashire Tramways" title, later changed to "Transport". Some printings had "A" or "S" at the foot to indicate Atherton or Swinton depot; "PB" for Platt Bridge appeared later.

Coloured tickets were re-introduced in the thirties: some were of normal size with 24 stages (4), but others were longer with 32 stages. The 1/2d. ticket with red overprint, a 'long' variety, remained in use until the change to machines, and was the only ticket of the 'overprint' style to do so. Some of the colours were 1d. white, 11/2d. yellow, 2d. salmon, 21/2d. blue, 3d. pink, 4d.brown or grey, 5d. purple, 6d. orange.

Day return tickets were widely introduced in 1933 and following years: these were coloured like single tickets but were longer and bore a red overprinted "R": workmen's tickets of the same design but with an overprinted "W" (7) were introduced at the same time. Whereas the day return tickets were lettered "South Lancashire Transport Company", the Workmen's tickets were lettered "S.L.T. Co. - L.U.T. & P. Co, Ltd."

Normal practice was to punch these tickets on issue to indicate the date of the month as well as the stage, and cancel them on the return journey to indicate the hour, the figures 1 to 6 and 7 to 12 appearing across the ends of the ticket for this purpose. Latterly the "R" overprint was not used, although "W" was retained.

On the joint trolleybus service to St. Helens the tickets were replicas of St. Helens Corporation design (8), long tickets in which those for values ending in halfpence were white with a coloured stripe corresponding to the colour of the ticket for the penny below.

An unusual ticket issued in the twenties also covered admission to "the Pit, Hippodrome, Leigh". There was, for instance, a white ticket with diagonal red hatching, covering the return journey, "Punch Bowl to Leigh Market", and admission to the cinema as above, all for 6d.

Lancashire United converted in the late thirties to 'TIM' ticket machines (manufactured by Ticket Issuing Machines Ltd., of Cirencester, and familiar to most readers as the type on which the value is set by a dial similar to a telephone dial), but the S.L.T. did not follow until about 1948, though the tickets issued by these machines were all lettered for both companies and had made occasional appearances on trolleybuses before that date. For a few years longer, trolleybuses running from the depot to Four Lane Ends or vice versa, to spend the day operating on the Bolton local service, continued to use the old tickets on these depot journeys. This avoided having an S.L.T. ticket machine lying idle on the vehicle all day while it was operating entirely in Bolton territory. Some values also remained in use for a while on Bolton Corporation motor-buses running between Walkden and Moses Gate on service 42, until Bolton too, went over to TIM machines. Latterly only the 1/2d. ticket was in use in this way - still the 'overprint' variety - after the 1/2d. fare had disappeared in Bolton itself.

As mentioned previously, there were no through bookings at Four Lane Ends until motor-buses replaced trolleybuses on the dissolution of the S.L.T. Conductors on the Leigh-Bolton service, therefore, always had two ticket racks, and Bolton Corporation tickets were used between Bolton and Four Lane Ends. After passing Four Lane Ends in either direction, the conductor would work through the vehicle afresh, issuing another ticket to each passenger. After the S.L.T. had converted to machines, Bolton Bell Punch tickets remained in use between Bolton and Four Lane Ends until about 1952, some time after Bolton had converted to machines on all its own vehicles. When stocks of Bolton tickets were virtually exhausted, there came a conversion to machines on this section as well. S.L.T. conductors now changed machines at Four Lane Ends. However, S.L.T. not Bolton, machines were used. To avoid confusion, the machines used on the Bolton side were distinguished by a large painted "BC", and distinctive

ticket rolls were used, with a green stripe on both edges throughout the roll. This was necessary not only to distinguish the areas, but also because tickets on this route were valid for free transfer to Trinity Street station, Bolton, whereas tickets on L.U.T. routes into Bolton were not; and of course the TIM tickets were lettered for both companies. Incidentally, the L.U.T. and S.L.T. originally used red ink in their TIM machines, but changed to blue about the end of the war, as did many other operators. The change to machines also did away with special tickets for the Atherton-St. Helens route, although St. Helens Corporation used green paper in their machines on that service.

On the through services at Moses Gate, through jointly-titled tickets existed for the most common bookings (10), but a few cross-boundary passengers had to re-book; however even where passengers required two tickets it was customary to issue both at once. For bookings entirely in S.L.T. territory on these routes, S.L.T. tickets were used, and it is curious to note that these remained in use on trams sometime after S.L.T. ceased to run any trams of its own. While ordinary S.L.T. tickets with numerical stages were used on the Walkden section, the *Black Horse* section had S.L.T. tickets of a form resembling the 1910 design, still in use in the 1940s: there was a 1d. orange ticket in the second 'geographical' design, with a corresponding 1 1/2d. workmen's return (yellow) and 1d. child return (green), and a purple exchange ticket: for whereas the S.L.T. normally only cancelled returns, Bolton issued Exchange tickets for them, and so this special ticket was devised for Bolton trams in S.L.T. territory.

The through joint services to Salford, introduced in the late twenties, had only a few cross-boundary bookings, most passengers having to re-book; the special jointly-titled through tickets (11) were of the 'geographical' style. For the ceremonial last trolleybus on 1st September 1958, a large (4 1/2 inches by 2 inches) white card ticket, with gilt edges, and printed in red, was produced. The stage headings were "IN 1900" and "OUT 1958" but unfortunately there was a misplaced apostrophe in the title of the centre column: "58 year's service".

Farnworth U.D.C.

The first tickets were in rolls, perforated, and were printed by Bibby, Warburton, and Co. According to contemporary newspaper reports, there were four values: these would obviously be 1/2d. 1d., and 1 1/2d., single. and 1d. workmen's return.

Soon there came a change to conventional tickets in nailed pads: a 1/2d. pink ticket is known, printed by Williamson, lettered on the left "UP - Longcauseway Crossing to Worsley Road", and on the right "DOWN - Worsley Road to Longcauseway Crossing". However, between these two issues there was an issue of roll tickets printed by Williamson.

Appendix II. The Liverpool and Prescot Light Railway

Of the various lines proposed by the Lancashire Light Railways Co., Ltd., the Liverpool and Prescot Light Railway was the only one ever constructed by that Company. Financially, of course, it was closely linked with the South Lancashire Tramways Company, by virtue of the common ownership of the two companies, but for operational purposes it was virtually a part of the St. Helens tramways. A provisional Light Railway Order was obtained in May 1898 and confirmed by the Board of Trade on 10th March 1899. Certain legal advantages were gained by obtaining powers under the Light Railway Acts rather than the Tramways Act. The line was 3 miles 9 chains in length, laid entirely as a street tramway along the main Liverpool and Prescot Road from the then Liverpool city boundary at Berry's Bridge, Knotty Ash, to Brook Bridge, Prescot. The St. Helens tramway extension from the *King's Arms*, the former steam tram terminus, in the centre of Prescot, 44 chains to Brook Bridge, was opened in January 1901 (the exact date cannot be traced). At the time the Liverpool & Prescot Light Railway Order had been applied for, this extension was only a proposal; it was authorised by an Act of 19th August 1898.

The route of the Liverpool and Prescot Light Railway now lies through an almost completely built-up area, with only a few glimpses of open countryside, but at the time it was built, there were only a few scattered houses over its whole length and local traffic was practically non-existent. The greater part of the line lay in what is now the Urban District of Huyton-with-Roby; its population of 55,783 in 1951 represented an increase of 973% since 1931, which was little changed from that of twenty or thirty years earlier.

As originally planned, the Liverpool and Prescot was to have passing loops only every half mile, but in fact a number of additional loops were constructed, amounting in total to 46 chains. It had been intended to build a depot on the south side of the road at Woolfalls Bridge, but by the time construction was started in 1901 the L.L.R. Company was closely associated with the New St. Helens company, having several directors in common, and it was natural that arrangements should be made for the St. Helens company to be responsible for the operation of the line and the manning, stabling, and maintenance of its cars.

The line was complete six months before it opened; it was inspected in April 1902. It was laid with 86-lb rail, the sharpest curve was 50ft radius, and the steepest gradient 1 in 20. The British Insulated Wire Co., had not only supplied and erected the overhead equipment but also supplied current from its Prescot works. Rather elaborate waiting rooms were built at the principal stopping places.

The opening was several times postponed, the delay being blamed on Liverpool Corporation who were constructing an extension from Old Swan to Knotty Ash. When this was nearly complete, it was announced that the Liverpool and Prescot would open on Monday 23rd June 1902, but the opening was postponed slightly. A service was operated throughout Tuesday afternoon to allow the tram crews to become familiar with the road, and passengers were carried. The proper advertised service began on Wednesday 25th June. A through service was provided between St. Helens and Knotty Ash. It ran every 15 minutes, starting at 6.00 a.m. from St. Helens, and the journey time was 45 minutes. The last cars left St. Helens at 10.15 p.m. and Knotty Ash at 11.00 p.m. The fare from St. Helens to Knotty Ash was $6^{1}/_{2}$d. single, 9d. return. The single fare was soon reduced to 6d., and in July 1904 to 5d. On the Light Railway itself, the original fare from Brook Bridge to Knotty Ash was 3d., with intermediate 1d. stage points at *Blue Bell Inn* and Horn Smithies (Page Moss). On 1st October 1902 special through excursion bookings were introduced from St. Helens (2/-) and Prescot (1/9) to Southport (Lord Street station), changing from the tram to the Cheshire Lines Committee's trains at Knotty Ash: the ticket also included the half-mile journey by Liverpool Corporation tram from the end of the Light Railway at Berry's Bridge, Knotty Ash, to Knotty Ash and Stanley station.

Although the St. Helens company actually operated the cars on the Light Railway, and provided the crews, seven cars were owned by the L.L.R. and numbered in the St. Helens fleet.

A through tram service was introduced on Monday 18th May 1903 between St. Helens and Liverpool Pier Head. It ran every half hour between noon and 10.00 p.m. There were no through bookings at first, but a through ticket was introduced later between the two termini (a distance of $12^{1}/_{2}$ miles) at 9d. single, 1/3d, return. The service was operated only by L.L.R. cars, and Liverpool Corporation crews worked the cars between Knotty Ash and Liverpool. The through service ceased on Wednesday 13th December 1905, but through tickets continued to be issued for several years.

Liverpool Corporation cars did, however, work over the line from time to time. It is believed that a Liverpool car was occasionally despatched to St. Helens at holiday times if crowds of would-be passengers built up at Pier Head in the evening. Liverpool cars also worked through on various special occasions. For instance, when the new reservoir near Eccleston Lane Ends, between Prescot and St. Helens, was opened in 1904, a special car came through from Liverpool. On 29th September the same company, and by the existence of the holding company, South Lancashire Electric Traction & Power. On the other hand, the impression could well have arisen because the cars bore the title "South Lancashire Tramways Company" on the side. Of course, it can be argued that the St. Helens Watch Committee would have had to license the S.L.T. cars, and on subsequent occasions there are mentions of licences being granted to "South Lancashire cars". However, the L. & P. did open, with whatever cars were used, and no licences were issued until March 1903. This seems far more likely to result from assurances that the first lot of cars were only in temporary use, than from delay by the Watch Committee, who otherwise were usually prompt in licensing, but in the early days were not as strict as they later became about temporary use of 'foreign' cars.

One objection to the theory that operation began with S.L.T. cars on loan is that the 83-89 class of the S.L.T. are reported as Milnes cars, and these were of course the L. & P. cars, transferred to the S.L.T. in 1919. But the only basis for this claim is a fleet list supplied by the S.L.T.

nearly twenty years after tramway operation had ceased, and in one or two other respects, as already mentioned, this list has proved to be incorrect. In the absence of any photograph of the S.L.T.'s 83-89 class - even one photograph would probably settle the whole question - I would suggest that these were in fact the B.E.C. cars. Their non-standard nature in the S.L.T. fleet would account for their fairly quick withdrawal there.

These B.E.C. cars, whenever they may have operated on the L. & P., certainly existed. They had four-window bodies, with small ventilators above the windows. They were open-top with Milnes (!) 'exhibition' stairs. The upper-deck decency boards reached only to seat level and were surmounted by railings. The short canopies were included within the upper deck rails. The head lamp was on the canopy. The cars were rather narrow; the rocker panels were almost straight. Yet they had 'two and two' transverse seats on the upper deck (some reports say on the lower deck also, for 22). Total seating capacity was said to be 55. The cars were on B.E.C. 'SB-60' trucks, and had Westinghouse motors and controllers.

Plate 84. Ex-Farnworth bogie-car No.56 follows a single-truck car as it works the Leigh-Bolton route.

Appendix III. The Projected Bolton, Turton, and Darwen Light Railways

Even for a scheme prepared at the height of the 'Tramway Mania', the Bolton, Turton and Darwen scheme was incredibly optimistic. The plans were deposited on 30th November 1900 by the Lancashire Light Railways Co., Ltd., but although the application later received the formal approval of the Board of Trade, the powers were never confirmed. The S.L.E.T. & P. Co., was having too much difficulty in raising capital for the S.L.T. lines in the more populous industrial area of South Lancashire to concern itself further with a moorland line separated from the rest of the tramways it controlled, and the application for the B.T. & D. was allowed to lapse.

The total length of the Bolton, Turton and Darwen Light Railways was to be 9 miles 26 chains. Although Light Railway applications, unlike Tramway applications, do not specify the amount of double and single track, it appears from the details of the estimates prepared that double track would amount to 1 mile 69.55 chains. The estimated cost was £50,726.0s.3d.

Starting by an end-on junction with the Tongé Moor line of Bolton Corporation at the *Royal Oak*, Bradshaw, the main line would have extended, as an ordinary street tramway, along the main Bolton and Blackburn Road for 6 miles 27.65 chains (of which 1 mile 14.55 chains double track) to an end-on junction with the Darwen Corporation Tramways at their Cemetery terminus.* The commencement of the line was 359 feet above sea level; the Darwen terminus was at 702 feet, and the highest point, about four miles from the start, would be 917 feet. It follows that the gradients would have been severe, not so much in their steepness as in their length. From Tonge Moor through Bromley Cross, Egerton, and Dimple to the summit was an almost uninterrupted climb at steeper than 1 in 40, including half a mile at 1 in 25 or steeper. The maximum gradients were two lengths of about 200 yards each at 1 in 19½. From the summit there was over a quarter of a mile falling at 1 in 31 and 1 in 26, followed by a climb at 1 in 80 and a sharp fall, including a short distance at 1 in 15, to the Darwen boundary near Cadshaw. In Darwen the line climbed first at an average of 1 in 40 to a summit of 895 feet at Cadshaw farm, and then descended for the last mile at gradients between 1 in 20 and 1 in 33, with two short lengths even steeper: 1 in 16½ and 1 in 19.7. The track in Darwen, for the 1 mile 46 chains from the boundary to the Cemetery, was to be laid with a third rail to accommodate the four-foot gauge trams of Darwen Corporation. The Corporation can have had little reason other than civic pride for insisting on this third rail as the price of their co-operation, for there was nothing more than a few scattered houses all the way from the Cemetery to the boundary, and indeed for the next two miles to Dimple.

There were to be three branches from the 'main line'. The first, only 24.40 chains long, was to be to Bromley Cross station; leaving the main line at the *Volunteer Inn*, it ran due east on private right of way for 17.40 chains and then ran northwards along Railway Street and into the goods yard. The present Bromley Cross Road follows the then proposed private right of way.

The second branch provided a second connection with Bolton Corporation's system. From an end-on junction with the latter. at Dunscar Bridge, it was to run along Blackburn Road for 39.80 chains, almost entirely climbing at 1 in 24, to join the main line south of Egerton. 12 chains were to be double.

The third branch was the most curious of the lot; in its whole length of 2 miles 14.15 chains, there were scarcely half a dozen houses in sight after leaving the village of Egerton. Leaving the main line at Longworth Lane, in the centre of Egerton, the line was to run roughly westwards along Longworth Lane, across the moors, to finish at an un-named spot about half a mile short of the village of Belmont. For the first quarter mile to Delph Brook it was to fall at 1 in 26/27, with a short length of 1 in 17; the bridge over Delph Brook is at 596 feet above sea level, and from there the line climbed to 889 feet just short of its proposed terminus. The climb, however, was not continuous, and there were several rises and falls at 1 in 23 and 1 in 25. From Delph Brook to the terminus the line was to be laid not in the roadway but on the grass verge - on the north side as far as the two-mile point, and then on the south side. Just before Delph Brook, a rectangular plot of land roughly two acres in extent was to be purchased on the north side of the road; and at the terminus an irregularly-shaped field of about six acres was also to be purchased. Presumably these plots of land were intended for the construction of depots or of a depot and a power station, but although the rectangular plot at the Egerton end is easily understandable, being in a central situation for the B.T. & D. as a whole, the larger plot at the end of the Belmont branch is difficult to understand. It would be very inconveniently situated either as a depot or a power station, and there would be no convenient water-supply for the latter purpose.

The B.T. & D. Light Railways cannot ever have hoped to carry much passenger traffic: local traffic was bound to be small, and through traffic would obviously prefer the train to the tram. As the prospectus speaks of establishing "through communication from the Ship Canal to Accrington" it must be assumed that it was hoped to

This line, electrified on 1st December 1900, was part of the former Blackburn and Over Darwen steam Tramway.

Appendix V.Summary of Opening and Closing Dates

Summary of opening and closing dates

This summary is intended only for quick reference; further details, including through services to other undertakings, will be found in the text. The dates given are those of the first and last days of public service.

	First electric tram	Last electric tram
LEIGH-BOLTON LINE:		
Four Lane Ends - Leigh	20.10.02	16.12.33
Leigh Lowton Old Terminus	20.10.02	16.12.33
Lowton Old Terminus - Lowton St. Mary's	6. 7.06	16.12.33
HAYDOCK LINE:		
Atherton - Hindley	7. 2.03	2. 8.30
Hindley - Ashton	4. 4.03	2. 8.30
Ashton Haydock	4. 4.03	20. 6.31 (2)
SWINTON LINE:		
Atherton - Tyldesley	25.10.02	18. 8.31
Tyldesley - Boothstown	20.4.05	18. 8.31
Boothstown - Worsley - Swinton-Walkden	27.9.06	18. 8.31
Walkden Little Hulton - Buckley Lane	28.8.13	18. 8.31
FARNWORTH & KEARSLEY LINES: (3)		
Moses Gate - Black Horse (8)	13.4.00 (1)	12.11.44 (1)
Moses Gate - Albert Rd. - Brookhouse	9.1.02 (5)	12.11.44 (1)
Longcauseway	9.1.02 (5)	18. 8.31
Black Horse - Spindle Point	20.2.02 (5)	7.6.31
Spindle Point - Unity Brook	13.5.02 (5)	7.6.31
CLIFTON LIGHT RAILWAY:		
Unity Brook - Newtown	28.2.07	7.6.31
OTHER BRANCHES:		
Bag Lane, Atherton	25.10.02	before 1926
Worsley - Winton boundary.	29. 3.07	7.10.36) (7)
Walkden - Brookhouse	29. 6.06	12.11.44 (1)
Market St., Hindley (4)	21. 4.28 (6)	28. 2.31 (6)

(1)	Bolton Corporation	(5)	Farnworth U. D. C.
(2)	St. Helens Corporation	(6)	Wigan Corporation
(3)	Taken over by S.L.T. 1.4.06	(7)	Salford Corporation
(4)	Former steam tramway	(8)	Former horse tramway

Appendix VI. Selected Statistics

The mileage and passenger statistics which follow are extracted from the Official Returns of the Board of Trade - from 1919, the Ministry of Transport. It will be noticed that there are some inexplicable variations in the route mileages, which can only be accounted for by lack of consistency in including short connecting curves, in reckoning one-way tracks in parallel streets as one length of double or two lengths of single track, and in dealing with such problems as the length of double track where one was owned by Farnworth and one by Kearsley. In some cases an error is obvious: for instance in 1928 to 1930 the length in Hindley newly leased to Wigan has been subtracted from the mileage owned by the S.L.T. It should be noted that after 1919 lines owned by the S.L.T but worked by another undertaking are not included in the S.L.T. totals until the S.L.T. ceased to operate tramways itself: this accounts for the decrease in 1920, and also explains the increase in 1928 when the S.L.T started to participate in operation of the Ashton-Haydock section. Other variations are not easily explained. Some of the amomalies have been discussed in the text, but no attempt has been made here to correct even known errors, nor to convert milages into one set of units: they have been left in miles and chains, or miles and decimals of miles, as originally published.

The returns were not published during the First or Second World Wars, and publication of detailed statistics of individual undertakings was not resumed until after the Second War, so the last figures available are for 1937. The year-end adopted for the purpose of Returns was changed in 1903, so there is an overlap between the two sets of figures quoted.

In 1924 and subsequent years, there are two sets of figures in any years when there was inter-running with other undertakings. The first represents the car-miles operated, or passengers carried, by the undertaking's own cars , irrespective of where operated; the figures in brackets represent the car-miles operated, and passengers carried, on the company's track, irrespective of the ownership of the cars.

The figure of "net receipts", of course, represents the operating surplus; it does not take into account interest and similar charges, and cannot be equated with"profit".

Plate 86
. Bolton tramcars continued to work the former Farnworth route to Walkden until 1944, by which time the condition of the track was causing concern. Bolton car No.15 stands at the Walkden terminus in Bolton Road in June 1937, displaying the route letter F as used on the Farnworth and Walkden service.

Liverpool and Prescot Light Railway

Year ending	Car - miles operated	Passengers carried	Net receipts	Route miles owned	No. of cars
30. 6.03	165,364	751.370	£1,754	3m.9ch	7
31.12.03	187,996	681,266	£ 252	3m.9ch	7
31.12.04	182,834	765,960	£ 837	3m.9ch	7
31.12.05	181,173	708,265	£ 185	3m.9ch	7
31.12.06	177.038	744,299	£ 418	3m.9ch	7
31.12.07	106.237*	455,389*	£1,318	3m.9ch	7
31.12.08	110,324*	492,035*	£1,768	3m.9ch	7
31.12.09	108,060*	493,037*	£1,725	3m.9ch	7
31 .12.10	111,411 *	496,358*	£1,585	3m.9ch	7
31.12.11	107,498*	516,133*	£2,325	3m.9ch	7
3112.12	104,570	527,721	£2,051	3m.9ch	x
31.12.13	104,626	575,054	£2,023	3m.9ch	7

* Estimate. x Left blank: presumably printer's error. The figures for the year to 30.6.02 (which would in any case represent only one week's traffic) are not available.

South Lancashire Transport Company: Trolley Vehicles

Year ending	Vehicle miles operated	Passengers carried	Net receipts	ROUTE MILES				No. of vehicles
				Owned	Leased	Worked	Running powers	
31.12.30	181,166	1,295,507	£ 3,673	7.86	-	-	-	10
31.12.31	753,686 (751.270)	5,269,403 (5,261,462	£14,146	21.92	0.83	-	4.15	30
31.12.32	1,235,332 (1,234,8751	8,642.219 1 8,669.996)	£ 9,309	21.92	0.83	-	4.15	30
31.12.33	1,253,435 (1,248,719)	8,687,235 (8,644.803)	£10,395	26.66	0.83	3.21	4.15	46
31.12.34	2,070,068 (1.748,250)	15,718,386 (12,176,232)	£18,077	26.66	0.83	3.21	4.15	46
31.12.35	2,075,630 (1,789,219)	16,225,923 (12,803,727)	£26,426	26.66	0.83	3.21	4.15	47
31.12.36	2,212,483 (1,812,916)	19,020.097 (13,848,739)	£26,778	26.66	1.63	3.11	4.15	51
31.12.37	2,279,714 (1,839,346)	21,209,797 (15,284,192)	£28,682	26.66	1.74	3.11	4.15	53

Farnworth Council Tramways

Year ending	Car miles operated	Passengers carried	Net receipts	Route Miles Owned	Leased	No of cars
30.6.03	252,701	1,681,249	£2,002	2m.53ch	1m.78ch	7
31.3.04	242,524	1,532,293	£1,125	2m.53ch	1m.78ch	13
31.3.05	239,176	1,474,751	£1,812	2m.54ch	1m.78ch	13
31.3.06	219,765	1,494,924	£3,009	2m.54ch	1m.78ch	13

Earlier figures not available

South Lancashire Tramways Company - Tramways

Year ending	Car-miles operated	Passengers carried	Net receipts	Route miles			No of cars
				Owned	Leased	Total	
30. 6.03	641,301	6,985,969	£ 5,821	19m.38ch	nil	19m.38ch	46
31.12.03	1,117,939	5,445,462	£ 2,501	19m.38ch	nil	19m.38ch	46
31.12.04	1,230,758	5,864,959	£ 1,016	19m.38ch	nil	19m.38ch	46
31.12.05	1,211,038	5.955,794	£ 925	21m.50ch	nil	21m.50ch	46
31.12.06	1,599,176	8,199,998	£ 3,214	30m.53ch	4m.52ch	35m.25ch	82
31.12.07	2,094,504	10,443,445	£ 5,541	30m.53ch	6m.4ch	36m.57ch	82
31.12.08	2,134,020	12,062,558	£ 7,599	30m.53ch	6m.4ch	36m.57ch	82
31.12.09	2,147,608	12,954,754	£ 5,259	30m.53ch	6m.4ch	36m.57ch	82
31.12.10	2,161,354	13,258,971	£ 1,875	30m.53ch	6m.4ch	36m.57ch	82
31.12.11	2,059,793	13,777,769	£11,899	30m.53ch	6m.4ch	36m.57ch	82
31.12.12	2,014,598	13,976,742	£22,145	30m.53ch	6m.4ch	36m.57ch	82
31.12.13	2,092,457	14,885,653	£30,259	32m.40ch	6m.48ch	39m.8ch	82
31.12.19	2,092,213	25,957,995	£44,175	32m.40ch	6.68m.	39.18ch	89
31.12.20	1,994,985	23,940,840	£40,167	30m.59ch	6m.18ch	36m.77ch	89
31.12.21	1,920,976	21,867,678	£33,163	30m.59ch	6m.18ch	36m.77ch	89
31.12.22	1,945,612	20,104,057	£40,177	30m.59ch	6m.18ch	36m.77ch	89
31.12.23	1,942,035	19,859,833	£48,526	30m.59ch	6m.18ch	36m.77ch	89
31.12.24	1,879,144 (1,884,189)	20,206,978 (20,171,267)	£48,168	29.5m.	6.22m.	35.72m.	74
31.12.25	1,905,692 (1,910,088)	20,018,321 (19,840,314)	£44,669	29.18m.	6.22m.	35.40m.	74
31.12.26	1,877,681 (1,930,759)	17,560.995 (17,947,206)	£38,048	29.18m.	6.22m.	35.40m.	74
31.12.27	2,049,190 (2,060.364)	19,951,061 (19,200,187)	£37,918	29.18m.	6.52m.	35.70m.	76
31.12.28	2,065,326 (2,100,973)	19,468,970 (18,883,202)	£29,101	30.63m.	6.54m.	37.17m.	76
31.12.29	2,119,169 (2,100517)	19,347,825 (18,310,867)	£24,401	30.63m.	6.54m.	37.17m	76
31.12.30	1,843,286 (1,893,505)	16,521,648 (16,141,540)	£17,465	22.77m.	6.54m.	29.31m.	62
31.12.31	1,240,158 (1,273,322)	11,366,658 (11,421,479)	£25,301	8.22m.	2.17m.	10.39m.	24
31.12.32	739,332 (738,964)	7,224,507 (7,124,981)	£27,254	8.22m.	2.17m.	10.39m	23
31.12.33	701,778 (712,569)	6,737,885 (6,663,837)	£23,105	1.70m.	2.23m.	3.93m.	24
31.12.34	263,147	(3,319,837)	£5,646	1.70m.	2.23m.	3.93m.	0
31.12.35	263,304	(3,304,757)	£3,341	1.70m.	2.23m.	3.93m.	0
31.12.36	268,165	(3,674,754)	£5,966	1.70m.	2.23m.	3.93m.	0
31.12.37	268,350	(3,821,021)	£6820	1.01m.	2.23m.	3.24m.	0

Other books by Triangle Publishing:-

Trafford Tramways by Arthur Kirby.
  An account of the tramways in Sale, Stretford and Altrincham operated by Manchester over the period 1903 to 1946 contains 122 b&w photographs illustrating all aspects of the services. This unique record is complete with detailed track plan and fare table adjusted for inflation. Size 272 x 215mm. Card cover in colour, 64pp and priced at £10.95. ISBN 0 9529333 9X

The Last Whistle by Tom Pike.
  A nostalgic look back at Patricroft MPD and a brief history from the early days until closure in 1968. Features a number of photographs by Patricroft's most famous personality, Jim Carter. 64pp, 172 x 230mm, card cover, 75 b&w illustrations, shed plan and two O/S maps. Priced at £8.95
ISBN 0 9550030 08

SPARKS by Charles Buchanan.
  Sub-titled *A Celebration of British AC Electric Locomotives.* Beginning with the conversion of the former G.W. gas turbine No18100 and its introduction as a test loco, right through the AL1-AL6 series, classes 87, 89, 90, 91 and 92. All 25kv routes covered. Complete fleet lists. Laminated colour jacket, size 210 x 260, 176pp, 269 illustrations in colour and b&w. Priced at £21.95 ISBN 0 9550030 16

A Trolleybus to the Punch Bowl by P.J.Taylor.
With headquarters at Howe Bridge, Atherton, the overhead wires of the South Lancashire Transport Cos. trolleybus system traversed a large area of industrial Lancashire connecting the towns of Bolton, Farnworth, Swinton, Leigh and St. Helens, with the system's hub at Atherton. Commencing in 1930 the trolleybuses of the SLT faithfully served the regions cotton and mining communities until final demise in 1958. Long gone but fondly remembered, the reader is invited to experience once more *A Trolleybus to the Punch Bowl* as the author describes each route in the fashion that only a dedicated enthusiast can.
Lavishly illustrated with 394 plates including 8pp in full colour. Size A4, 200pp, hardback with full colour jacket. Large fold-out map, T.Ts, full history.
Priced at £32.00 ISBN 0 9529333 73

Plodder Lane for Farnworth by Bert Holland.
  The arrival of the L&NWR at Plodder Lane, its development over the years, and its eventual decline are all dealt with in detail, together with presentation of 114 b&w photographs of the area and many detailed maps of all the railway sites from Roe Green to Atherton that were operated by engines from Plodder Lane.
160pp, size 210 x 260, hardback with full colour jacket. Priced at £18.95 ISBN 0 9529333 65
This will become the standard reference work for Plodder Lane.